For Black Men Trying to Survive and Thrive in America

A Defense Attorney's Advice and Life Experiences

Ali Andrew Shakoor

<u>DEDICATION</u>

This book is dedicated to my family and my people, my race, whom I love so dearly.

"Keep some sunshine on your face."

Mudbone (Richard Pryor)

For Black Men/Ali Shakoor

CONTENTS

INTRODUCTION

For Black Men/Ali Shakoor

INTRODUCTION

I Am Here to Help My People

I am a forty-four-year-old black man. I grew up and survived under institutional racism in the United States of America. I am fortunate to be alive, free, and not without failures, but with a knowledge base to help young black men avoid incarceration. Over the years, I have spent a lot of time going in and out of jails and prisons. My entire legal career has been devoted to criminal defense; first as a public defender for three years, and for the last eleven years as an attorney representing indigent clients on death row in the state of Florida. Based on my experience, I know there is an easier way to live life than sitting behind bars like a wild animal that needs to be contained. I believe life is a one-shot movie. There is no rewind or restart when sentenced to death, or life in prison without a chance in hell for parole. Few men are ever released to start over again. Spending any amount of time in prison is wasteful and it limits your chance of upward mobility in a free world. Leaving this world in a prison body bag to a family that has largely gotten over grieving years ago, is pathetic commentary. "He could have been…" "He used to be…." "If only he had……" What more can be said when the game is up?

There really are innocent men in prison and thousands are serving sentences that are too severe. For the most part, the men I meet in prison are not like the former Mississippi Freedom Riders willing to challenge Jim Crow laws. There is no great cause driving them like South Africa's Nelson Mandela, or Reverend Dr. Martin Luther King Jr. They are not Gandhi-like heroes. There was no civil disobedience that they participated in for the greater good of mankind. The men I meet in prison have sacrificed their own precious freedom for idiocy, greed and a lack of respect for themselves and others. They have conned people, lied and stolen what they could have earned. They have committed armed robberies and left behind badly beaten or dead bodies. The men I meet in prison are often murderers and many are absolutely guilty. They have battered their wives and girlfriends and have victimized the most helpless among us. The men I meet in prison have molested children, because they were also likely abused as children. It is sad and cyclical.

What I know for sure, is that many of the men, I meet in prison were born with an opportunity to become anything they wanted, but they took another path. My statements and profound concern do not mean that I never meet some likeable personalities that are easy-going, funny and brilliant. In another combination of circumstances these men, and I could have drinks and watch sports all day long. Every man has an element of decency and humanity within our character, when we let it show.

For some prisoners, and this is according to their stories, what caused them to be in their unfortunate predicaments, is that it was someone else's failure to get out the way of their perception of "keeping it real" and "getting some respect." Many of our conversations center on feeling disrespected or "I didn't do it" is whispered or is shouted with tears of despair and a crazed look from trying not to fall apart. If they are not already crazy, prison can put someone over the edge. There is not enough money to rob, or to murder someone over that is worth a man's freedom. It is difficult to fully understand how some of these men did not see where their life was headed before they arrived in that chair shackled and opposite mine.

I have met way too many talented, handsome black men that have done some preposterous stuff, when they could have chosen a better way to live, like getting an education or learning a trade. Or, they could have gotten a damn job, any job. Really, is not slapping together cheeseburgers at McDonalds or Burger King better than pressing license plates for pennies? Is not the freedom to pee and defecate in private, in one's own bathroom, worth challenging a migrant worker from Mexico for his job picking beans and tomatoes? Of course, it is. Most men I meet in prison decided to go down that path of self-destruction.

However, I am clearly aware of the obstacles that oppressive institutional racism has created for black men. I understand outsourcing of jobs and the scarlet letter of a felony record. These are obstacles that will be discussed in this book. But we black men must also make fundamental personal changes, while simultaneously fighting to change the race-based policies which have created systematic oppression and the mass incarceration of black men

How can I help our brothers, as I walk along side, or sit in a chair opposite a man that has willingly forfeited his freedom, his own life? I want very much for neither of us to be there on his behalf, in prison, the last place many of them will live on Earth.

Some of these guys began a life of crime as small-time drug dealers when they were teenagers, while the real drug kingpins were laughing and sitting beside a shimmering pool drinking a glass of expensive wine. Big-shots have money for their lawyers to persuade prosecutors and even judges to leave them to their craft. Why won't drug hauling teenagers wise up and realize that they are being used. 50Cent got his act together. Well, it took him being shot nine times and a hip hop lottery ticket, before he took charge of his life. Now, he is a rich, self-made, business tycoon sipping Vitamin Water alongside his own pool. Smart people do not allow themselves to be used like mules. They take charge of their own future; their own destiny.

I found this important piece of information to prove one of my points. "According to a new study from the American Civil Liberties Union, which tracked marijuana arrests by race and county in all 50 states and the District of Columbia, black and white Americans use marijuana at about the same rate. However, blacks are nearly four times more likely than whites to be arrested on charges of marijuana possession in 2010." This information proves another one of my points. Police officers are often more likely to take the pot and the money, and then send white kids home to their parents. Whereas black offenders get arrested, then face a biased court system, followed by juvenile detention centers, and eventually are placed in the system on probation or in the state penitentiary.

Inevitably, more and more states are arriving at the conclusion that pot should be legal. Hopefully, now with marijuana increasingly being prescribed for medicinal purposes, we are heading in the right direction. Still, this does not change the fact that incarceration for blacks is more likely with police officers targeting black people, especially black males. These inequalities must stop.

I have suspected for years that criminal activity for some men is a desperate need for a warm place in the dead of winter, and air-conditioning for families in sweltering summers. They feel the pressure to provide food, clothing, physical and mental health care for their loved ones. Prior generations also taught that criminal activity was the "only" way to guarantee a family income in some neighborhoods. Misplaced pride in not being able to provide for children that they love, is poorly leveraged against the risks of imprisonment or death. Prison is also, unfortunately, a way to escape taking responsibility.

Racist practices to achieve an unsavory end, by our government are also clearly to be blamed for our current crisis. Men in baggy prison grays, slouching like slaves at an auction for a prison warden who needs them incarcerated to get federal funding is a racket that must stop. They are handcuffed and shackled before mostly white judges who often look at them without seeing any kind potential. Next, the men are sent off to prison, working as free labor for products later sold in the American marketplace and overseas.

Prisoners I meet are the fathers of sons and daughters who need them at home. They have let down the women and children who love them. Over the years, I have met hundreds of crying mothers, grandmothers, sisters, aunts, daughters, wives, lovers, and mistresses. Not many fathers are weeping for these prisoners, because they are not present, and many have never been involved in their children's lives. These missing fathers are often the victims in a cycle of imprisonment and recidivism. In writing this book, I am trying to keep our black men out of the system.

Quick story: One Sunday evening a couple of years back, my wallet fell out of my pocket during an Uber ride. No credit card was lost, just a spare house key, home gate/gym access card which would cost $50.00 to replace, various frequent buyer cards, and about $100.00 in cash. I eventually tracked down my Uber driver's information, only to find out he had presumed the wallet belonged to his last and final fare of that same night. So, the Uber driver had given *my* wallet to some other dude, who was apparently ignoring the driver's calls and texts in his efforts to track down a return of the wallet to the rightful owner-*me*. The Uber driver eventually sent me the guy's information, but I was not about to risk getting shot in some sketchy neighborhood in a misguided quest to retrieve my property. I could have called the cops, but I hated the thought of getting some fool caught up in the criminal justice system over his greed and short-sightedness, or potentially shot by some reckless or deranged demon cop. I decided the greedy chump could keep the cash. I could chalk that up to the game or cost of doing business. I just wanted and needed the rest of the contents back.

Luckily, the Uber driver trusted my situation enough to provide me with information about the person who should have my wallet. I chose to call the phone number, as opposed to just showing up at the address. The young man immediately answered the phone and started claiming that he was staying at a friend's apartment, and someone there had accepted the wallet after he left. The residence was only 3.4 miles from my job. I decided to play the "lawyer" card and told him that I did not care who kept the cash, but I really would like the other items back. He seemed young and nervous. I also followed up with a text, making sure to memorialize the conversation. I wanted a paper trail, for my own safety. This is all I planned to do, in order to resolve the situation. I figured I would be more careful next time. On the storming night I left my wallet in the Uber, I was getting dropped off at a restaurant within walking distance to home. I must have been reckless in failing to secure my wallet deep in my pocket, before exiting into the rain.

I really was not about calling the cops and getting some young man caught up in the criminal justice system over some petty theft. Also, who knows what other illegality the cops may have discovered during their investigation? I was once young and made a lot of myopic mistakes. I figured I would just wear the "L" and do better next time. I, of course, wanted the culprit to do right by me and return my wallet. And, I hoped he was scared straight and appreciated the opportunity to not have the cops on his ass over a stupid decision.

Apparently, my negotiation skills were effective, because the dude texted back an address to meet at. I insisted on verifying it was a public place. I got off the couch and drove to a pizzeria in a poor urban area. Once I arrived, I texted the number to inform him that I was present and ready to retrieve my property. The dude texted me back stating that my wallet was left with the pizzeria manager. Yes, it was, and minus the cash and the club cards to my local neighborhood pub and Smokey Bones restaurant, but I got the wallet and keys back. I was ready to recreate the "Jules" to "Ringo" speech from Pulp Fiction about this precious wallet, but it is probably best that I never met anyone face-to-face, as it saved a lot of embarrassment and potential risk. It ended well; all things considered. And, I had made sure to "walk-the-walk" about helping young black men stay out of the system.

My full name is Ali Muhammad Andrew Shakoor. My life easily could have ended in a jail cell. But for the strength of family, some smart, calculated, decisions and a series of good fortune, I was spared a journey into the prison system. I have a good life. I am a post-conviction attorney in the State of Florida representing indigent capital defendants on death row. I was born in Toledo, Ohio, but I grew up primarily in Worthington, which is a suburb of greater Columbus, Ohio. I graduated from Worthington Kilbourne High School in 1993, and The Ohio State University in 1996, where I received a BA in Political Science. In 2003, I received my law degree from Capital University Law School, where I graduated Cum Laude. My mother is an accomplished author and business owner, Jordana Y. Shakoor. I have a younger sister, Keyomah Shakoor. Like my mother and I, my sister also received her under graduate degree from Ohio State. My sister remained at Ohio State to complete her studies, earning a Jurist Doctorate degree. My sister has two children, my niece and nephew whom I absolutely adore. I have a wise and feisty grandmother, Arella Jordan "Grannie" who inspires all of us with her knowledge and courage.

In this book, I am conversing directly to the reader. **For Black Men Trying to Survive and Thrive in America:** *A Defense Attorney's Advice and Life Experiences* is a discussion; words directly from me to my fellow black brothers. I give this advice while discussing my personal experiences navigating through oppressive American white supremacy, and always determined to avoid becoming another statistic in the prison system.

Chapter One

You Deserve a Great Life

When you were a child, what did you want to be when you grew up? Like many of you, I wanted to be a professional athlete or famous musician. But we all know that physical realities and limited opportunities will prevent many of us from achieving fame and fortune. So, let us keep it more basic and do not get me wrong, I want you to understand me clearly. If you have a talent that needs to be fostered, do that. Strive for your dreams. However, it is important to develop an educational foundation and a skill-set as part of a backup plan, just in case fame and fortune remains out of your grasp. Most importantly, make it dead set in your mind that you plan on living to be old, and that you do not want to be a part of the criminal justice system in the future.

Did you want to be a good parent? How about having a life where you never had to worry about where your next meal would come from or how the bills would get paid? I bet you wanted to grow up to be happy and healthy. These are the types of goals that are realistic and achievable. It's just a matter of getting your mind wrapped around the fact that not only do you deserve these options, but you are more than capable of making it happen.

For Black Men/Ali Shakoor

Learning to understand your need for self-worth starts with knowing where you come from. Being of African descent is something to cherish. There are none more talented and beautiful people on the planet than black people. That is not to say that we are "better", because inherently, all of humankind is created equal. I just want to stress that there is never, ever, a justification to feel inferior to anyone, for we are great.

The last leader of the free world, Barack Hussein Obama, is of second generation African decent and self-identifies as a black man, despite having a white mother. Whether excelling in sports, with the hopes of a country and billions of business dollars depending on us or exposing the essence of humanity when performing in the entertainment world, we matter. We are laborers, educators, professionals and all-around good citizens, as we matter. We are positively essential to the evolution of human kind and a part of everything that is good in this world. Love yourself and always maintain your self-respect.

This starts with the use of the word "nigger." Stop using it. Eliminate it from your thoughts as something that is worth protecting or "owning," I know it is ubiquitous in our culture. From the music, to our sense of humor, to the way we address each other in every day conversations, the word nigger is the most dominant word in black American culture. However, it has reached the point that society has evolved to where *we* are both policing and dictating the use of and defending the word as something to protect and value. This is ridiculous. It should stop.

Unfortunately, it is hard to change old habits. I did not reach this point of view in my life until sometime in 2013; right around the time George Zimmerman was acquitted for the murder of Trayvon Martin. As a lawyer, I can rationalize the acquittal. But the way that the case divided our country, and how I felt about the way young Martin's life was being treated as insignificant in the media and amongst certain demographics, the term nigger has become utterly unacceptable to me. The Trayvon Martin coverage was a huge turning point in my life and made me even more aware of what it means to be black in America.

We are also killing each other in urban communities at horrifying rates. When a young black man shoots another young black man in America's streets, the last thing he calls the fallen brother, probably ends in "nigger." It is a degrading display of self-hatred. Putting an "a" at the end of the word does not make it more useful. If so, we would accept the use of "nigga" by others outside of our race. It is silly to keep fighting for the use of the so-called "n word" and then also engaging in embarrassing double standards. This thought process is not for the benefit of white America. It is for our own personal growth. I roll my eyes when some whites, usually conservative, express feigned frustration about how whites can't use the word with the same open freedom of frequency as black people.

Yes, some white people suffer indignation over being forbidden from doing something that is allowable to blacks. That comes from a sense of white privilege and generationally ingrained arrogance. However, the ability to smugly mock whites for not having the freedom to say something that we may freely utter, is not worth the damage that the word does to our collective and personal psyche. The word has an ugly history and we don't have a use for it in any type of positive sense.

I understand that the word may have a use in the arts (literature, film, music), in the proper context, but it should always be looked upon as the pejorative term that it is, and always will be. The great comedian, Richard Pryor, likely used the word nigger more than anyone in the history of pop culture. He used it freely on talk shows, during his concert films, and even used the term as a title on a Grammy award winning comedy albums *This Nigger's Crazy* and *Bicentennial Nigger*. No entertainer had so proudly and boldly used the word. Eventually, Richard Pryor came to his senses. During his concert film, *Live on the Sunset Strip*, Richard Pryor explained why he would no longer use the word nigger after a trip to Africa that changed his perspective and world view: *"When I was in Africa, this voice came to me and said, 'Richard, what do you see?' I said, 'I see all types of people.' The voice said, 'But do you see any niggers?' I said, 'No.' It said, 'Do you know why? Cause there aren't any.'"*

For Black Men/Ali Shakoor

We are not "a nigga" or "niggers." Why? Because *there aren't any*. Simply try to use the word "brother" or "brotha" instead. Focus your mind to eliminate the word nigger/nigga from your vocabulary and you are well on your way to enhancing your sense of self-worth. And look, I know this is a divisive issue within our community. As a fan of hip hop music for over thirty years, I understand the prevalence of the term, and I express no desire to eliminate it from decades of outstanding musical output. I feel no shame in admitting that I will get excited and start getting charged up when "Down for my Niggaz" blasts out the speakers. That's just enjoying a piece of art, not making it a part of my everyday expressions about our people. I can bob my head along to Biggie's flow, just like I can appreciate the talents and charisma of Pacino playing Michael Corleone. These are characters in an art form. That being said, listening to a talented and wise legend like Jay Z use it unnecessarily and frankly, lazily and boring in an album opener like "Holy Grail" is disappointing. It is an epithet. Use it with care. The word is just something that needs to be past its time and place in everyday use, and it needs to be marginalized so that we can continue to progress as a people. We are amid a crisis, and some self-reflection and changes are in order. And the so-called "N-word" is simply more trouble than it's worth and holding us back.

Self-worth also applies to your physical appearance and health. There are plenty of ways to show personal expression, without waddling around with your ass hanging out of your pants. Walking around in public with your underwear showing is not swaggy, bout it, rebellious or cool. It is a sign of low self-esteem. The "style" is also long past played out; not that it was ever something to admire. I hope that it is out of style at the point when this book is published, and please don't allow something else just as disparaging to take its place.

Present yourself with a sense of pride and move on with your life with your head held high and your mind ready to conquer. Do not allow past errors in judgment or personal embarrassments define you. To those that roll their eyes at this paragraph as "heard it before," well you are reading it here as well, because I care about the empowerment of my people, and this starts with self-respect. Believe me; I understand that our problems in the black community are beyond this matter. I am fully aware of the oppressive factors--both historical and lingering--that white America has done to us. These matters will be addressed throughout this book. However, you can control how you choose to present yourself to the world. A sense of dignity is crucial, in navigating your way to a better life, and spite those demographics who aim to oppress you.

How is your health? A key way to insure you are maximizing your ability to give yourself a better life is by taking care of your health. I have personally dealt with health problems all my life. It seems that I was born with asthma. Then as an adult, I developed a weird problem with neuropathy in my limbs, but only on the left side. Doctors cannot find a reason for this slight weakness. But at one time this lingering neuropathy, asthma, and problems with my gastrointestinal system; it all negatively affected my personality. It is hard to focus on doing better when you do not feel well. Up until getting surgery for a partial hiatal hernia about seven years ago, I can recall being irritable and negative on a near daily basis. I was sick and self-pitying, moody, and spending too many countless hours arguing with strangers on online message boards. Yes, imagine taking time to get into silly fights on political blogs. So many wasted hours were spent exchanging insults and trying to get the ***last word.*** For what and for whom? I don't know. It was a waste of my life. My time most certainly should have been spent in more productive ways. I am still highly opinionated online and will engage in spirited debates, but it is a long way from going online for the sole purpose of exchanging insults and trolling. I was venting my frustration over all kinds of issues, until my health improved. My surgery was a success, and with the best medication, my asthma is finally under control. Nothing prevents me from doing what I want to do. Most days, I absolutely feel great. And, I work out several times a week. And, I can declare that with a positive mindset, my health has improved.

I shared this embarrassing information as an example of being able to acknowledge and grow from mistakes. If you are going through any health problems, or perhaps somebody close to you is ill or dying, the stress alone can alter and harm your entire personality. It is very crucial to take advantage of healthcare. Life is too precious and short to allow stubbornness or ignorance to prevent you from maximizing everything life can offer, so try to maintain quality health.

You have probably heard of a boxing legend by the name of Bernard Hopkins. Hopkins was born and raised on the dangerous and ugly streets of Philadelphia, PA. He was a street punk; a violent criminal throughout his teens. Before Hopkins matured into a full-grown man, he was convicted of multiple robberies by the age of seventeen. His sentence was for a maximum of eighteen years in prison, but with an opportunity for early parole. Now that was a time of definitive choice for Bernard Hopkins. What kind of future was he going to create for himself?

Instead of taking a route of absorbing new criminality during his prison stay and guaranteeing himself a dead-end future by becoming a sad cliché, Bernard learned and plotted while incarcerated. Hopkins learned boxing and self-discipline. During his five year stay in prison—paroled early for good behavior—Hopkins stayed out of trouble and turned his attention to boxing. As he strolled out of prison at age twenty-three and facing nine years of parole, the warden assured Hopkins that he would return. However, Bernard Hopkins assured himself that he would never return to that, or any state-run cage, ever again. While on parole, Hopkins stayed free of distractions and finished his parole stint while rising in the middleweight ranks to become the undisputed champion of the world. Hopkins finished a legendary career that saw him fighting at an elite level as he approached his fiftieth birthday. Bernard Hopkins is a living legend. He has also taken care of his finances in a responsible manner and has set himself up for a post-fight career as a promoter and boxing commentator. Hopkins is a great example of what a young black man can achieve if he takes the time to believe in and invest in himself, and by refusing to be defeated by a racist and oppressive society.

Sexual abuse, unfortunately, is often a taboo and unspoken topic in the black community; more so when it comes to young black male victims. The stigma can be devastating. Any type of child abuse, physical and emotional, can cause anger and resentment which can affect your inner self and cause one to aggressively unleash the pain on an unsuspecting outer world. It is important to seek mental health treatment to deal with the personal turmoil. This is not something to be ashamed about, rather it's heroic. In recent years, some well-known black men have revealed how they have overcome the struggles from past child sexual abuse.

Boxing great Sugar Ray Leonard is a sports hero. He won a gold medal for our country in the 1976 Olympics, and then he fought as one of the greatest pound-for-pound boxers of all time; winning titles in five divisions on his way to the Hall of Fame. Besides his talents in the ring, Sugar Ray was also a famous commercial pitch man. He was one of the dominant American pop culture icons of his era, and yet the whole time he was struggling with anger and guilt. Little did the public know that Leonard was wearing a mask, and secretly in the depths of substance abuse because his secrets were so burdensome. Sugar Ray Leonard was sexually abused as a teenager. Several years ago, he revealed that he was taken advantage of by one of his amateur boxing coaches, before he would go on to fight through this pain on his way to representing our great country in Montreal.

At the height of his legendary career as a champion and celebrity, Leonard was also secretly abusing drugs and alcohol. He was unhappy and no one was able to encourage him through his struggles. When he finally gained the courage to reveal everything to his wife at the time, he was unfortunately met with a woman too ill-equipped to offer the support, love and backbone that any great black man desperately needs from his woman. Times are different now, and this is due to the courage of men like Mr. Leonard, and the evolving standards of decency that drive our nation. In the past, particularly within our community, the subject of sexual abuse has been unspoken, taboo and cloaked in shame. That entire concept is sad and ridiculous. Every right-minded person understands that child sexual abuse is evil. The shame lies with the perpetrator, never the victim.

For Black Men/Ali Shakoor

If you have ever been victimized as a youth, do not let that trauma hinder your personal growth and development. Talk to somebody and unload your burden. Seek help. Besides Leonard, other brave men who have come forward with their stories, in hopes of helping others, include former college and pro basketball standout Kenny Anderson, media mogul Tyler Perry, and former NBA player Keyon Dooling. Those are just a few of many, too many, but learn from their strength of character. Respect and learn from their will to survive and help others.

You deserve a better life. You have paid your dues and earned it. Do not let negativity hold you back. To stay out of the criminal justice system, now is the time to start making better life choices and that starts with self-respect and loving yourself.

Chapter Two

<u>**Understanding Our Predicament**</u>

The incarceration rate for black males in this country is completely unacceptable. Black Americans make up approximately 13% of the U.S. population (http://quickfacts.census.gov/qfd/states/00000.html). However, black men constitute about 37% of the overall men in prison, followed by white men at 32% and then Hispanic men at 22%. (http://www.drugwarfacts.org/cms/Race_and_Prison#sthash.OZxemc hm.RHGDeorG.dpbs). A strong case can be made that this breakdown is no accident or unexplained phenomenon. For starters, everyone reading this book needs to purchase a copy of *The New Jim Crow*, by Michelle Alexander. Alexander's groundbreaking book explains in detail how this country's "War on Drugs" creates a caste system where the black urban community is stuck in a cycle of drugs, seemingly endless poverty, and incarceration.

You will hear people in society, usually conservatives, lament about the breakdown of the black family household. Where are the fathers? Why is there such a high unemployment rate? The fact of the matter is urban communities do not offer viable employment opportunities and this is due to government policies that promote the outsourcing of jobs, and a lack of financial investment in the inner cities. Black fathers often have few options if they live close to where they were raised; with scarce employment outside of the illegal drug trade, a lot of "fathers" are either in the throes of addiction, in prison, or dead.

The disinvestment of resources in urban areas along with the practice of "redlining," which restricts prospective black homeowners from buying into safer and thriving communities, essentially created what has been known over the years as the ghetto or "hood." Although such practices have been outlawed in explicit form, the recent Supreme Court decision <u>Texas Department of Housing and Community Affairs v. The Inclusive Communities Project, Inc</u>. (2015), shows the reality that such conduct is still carried out today through practices that create a disparate negative impact on blacks in urban areas. To achieve the "personal accountability" that is essential, though often dismissively thrown at our culture, you must study and understand these realities that create our circumstances.

In previous generations, black families had more options. I was raised by a single mother, who gave birth to me as an eighteen-year-old. My mother made sure my sister and I were raised in the suburbs and attended quality schools, even if we were among the poorer people in those communities. I am more a product of my mother and father's high school romance and my mother's poor choices in men, than from the direct results of the "War on Drugs." I am lucky that I was born when and where I was in 1974.If the birth dates of the previous three generations of my family lineage were pushed up a decade or so, I could be one of the casualties of the crack epidemic.

My mother was born in Greenwood, Mississippi. My grandparents raised her, along with four sisters in the heart of the Jim Crow south in the soul of the civil rights movement. Andrew L Jordan, my grandfather, was one of the early leaders in that movement. My grandfather was the Executive Secretary of the Leflore County Branch NAACP, in Greenwood, Mississippi. He was an associate of Medgar Evers and put his life and sanity on the line to protect the rights of black people, and to support his large family of seven. He was a vigilant and passionate leader. The following, is an excerpt from a speech hc gave at 32 years of age:

<u>NAACP at Mass Meeting Thursday – September 19, 1963.</u>

My fellow citizens, my heart bleeds when I see the diminutive degree of pride you take in freedom for yourselves, and your children. Are you so satisfied that you can afford to exclude yourself from the world-wide struggle for freedom? Are you so pleased with this situation until you can afford to allow your children to grow up in the same Jim Crow society as you have?

For Black Men/Ali Shakoor

It isn't enough to be well off yourself and allow your brother and sisters to suffer. It isn't enough to say the word ["] freedom ["] in a prayer or the word freedom in a song or freedom is what I crave for, and make no effort to achieve it.

We must not allow ourselves to be fooled by penny-Annie jobs to the extent that we become steadfast, and refrain from or disregard the proclivity of reality. We must not allow ourselves to think, because we are not participating actively in the movement, that we are respected or looked upon as having sound judgment by the white man.

We have had a movement going here over a year trying to awaken you to your responsibilities as citizens. Many of you have called the movement ["] mess, ["] and as a result refused to have anything to do with it.

We are not doing anything any different today from what Christ did during his life on earth over two thousand years ago. He was simply trying to awaken people to their responsibilities as citizens and those rights which belonged to them as citizens. There were people who called the mass meetings he held ["] mess ["] too. There were kings who felt that he was destroying their system of feudalism, and he was, because people began to flee from idolatry and seek something more [tangible].

The kings became angry and discontent just like the lily whites today and tried to make deals with him. He would not listen to deals, the same as we don't listen to deals. The kings then had him killed, but not because he was a member of the NAACP, SNCC, SCLC or CORE, he was killed because he was trying to teach the people the word of God and enlighten the poor people to the injustice had been imposed on them by the kings.

For Black Men/Ali Shakoor

Abraham Lincoln wasn't killed because he was a member of the NAACP, SNCC, SCLC or CORE, he was killed because he wanted all Americans to be free from slavery, for he knew that the nation could not survive with half slaves and half free.

Those children were killed while in Sunday School in Birmingham, they were not members of the NAACP, they were merely attending the House of God, exercising one of the first amendments of the constitution – the right to [worship] in a peaceful assembly.

Medgar Evers, the field secretary for the NAACP in Mississippi was killed because he wanted freedom for all his people. He gave his life for that cause, how about you helping to avenge our loss by continuing to push for what you know is right.

You see my fellow citizens; this is nothing new. There have been over four (4) thousand Negroes killed and mutilated in the South, 90 % being in Mississippi, since 1850. They were not Negroes who were identified as leaders, but Negroes like yourselves who so openly and thoughtlessly say [,] "I'm not going to have anything to do with that mess!"

You are involved my friends if you are black, and I presume you are. It is just a matter of time when some thoughtless illiterate pale-face throws a bomb into your window.

Don't allow this to happen before you decide to act. Prevent this by trying to do something for humanity toward achieving freedom and First-Class Citizenship. This can only be done through voter registration.

For Black Men/Ali Shakoor

Every teacher should be a preceptor in their teaching. If you don't believe in voting don't teach the students anything about it. On the other hand [,] if you do believe in voting, teach the students how to vote and vote yourself – there by you are being a precept of what you teach.

Many have asked what is the NAACP: The NAACP is many things; it is a [breakthrough] of segregation, it is a stool for a black man or woman to sit on in an all-white café, it is a seat for a black boy or girl in all white school, college and university. It is a key to a restroom marked for whites only, it is a [symbol] of justice in a white society, it is a resident in a white neighborhood, it is a key to equal job opportunities for Negroes based on his educational status and [preparation], rather than his pigmentation. It is a voice that cries out for freedom wherever it is lacking, it is a franchise to vote. Finally, it is an organization that has surpassed its prediction, but yet digging up the roots of injustice and transplanting the holes with justice, equity and [fair] play for all people regardless of creed or color.

Every Negro who loves freedom and hates injustice will join the NAACP. You are not [alone] in this fight. Every person who knows the effectiveness of the NAACP is a part of it through membership. Do yourself justice by joining the NAACP and support these movements and let's hurry and get this job done. The velocity by which freedom will come depends on every one of us. We can get it today if we decide within ourselves that we are going all out to demand it. We intend to slug it out, to fight right here on this home front if it takes the rest of our lives – until freedom is ours.

I am very proud of my grandfather's sense of advocacy and love for his race. By being so outspoken in the Jim Crow south, he was putting his life and his family's life in danger. He understood the

For Black Men/Ali Shakoor

significance of the right to vote. After the assassination of Medgar Evers in 1963, and increased threats on his own life, and due to his career prospects being thwarted because of his outspokenness, my grandfather decided to head up north to start a life that offered more freedom and opportunity. His older brother, Clevester Jordan, had established himself up there years before with a job and a home. My grandfather secured a factory job with Enterlake Iron and Toledo Shipbuilding, joining his older brother's family in Toledo, Ohio. Once he found a temporary residence to rent, my grandmother joined him shortly after escaping the oppressive South with their five daughters. My mother is the second oldest.

The fact that my grandfather had such an employment opportunity is a reflection on a time when northern inner cities offered something beyond drugs and danger. There truly used to be major manufacturing jobs in this country. These jobs, mainly available for men, supplied a quality wage that could support a household. The Enterlake Iron and Toledo Shipbuilding company was a job that required long hours and hard labor, and my grandfather, along with his coworkers was up to the task until he could acquire a teaching position in the Toledo Public School System which he did rather quickly in the mid-'60s. In 1978, the Enterlake Iron and Toledo Shipbuilding Company closed, and along with it, there was closure and elimination of career opportunities for dozens of families. The building was demolished in 1986 around the same time that the crack epidemic was taking a strangle hold in urban areas all around the country.

Before getting into the flood of crack in urban black communities, let's consider why there is even a nationwide establishment of areas known as "urban black communities." My grandfather, after escaping to the north and ultimately continuing his teaching career, almost lost the family's first home at one point.

The following brief story would seem farfetched in a Hollywood movie, but the facts are indisputably true.

While struggling to raise his large family, and even after securing a second job, my grandfather fell behind on his mortgage payments. Through long hours and demonstrating the strong work ethic that he was known for, he managed to save enough money to bring the payments up to date. However, the lending company refused to accept the payments and attempted to foreclose on the family's middle-class suburban home. A court date was set to facilitate the foreclosure process. Out of anger and desperation, my grandfather did what he was bred to do. He fought for justice. He took the time to write a heartfelt letter and addressed it to the President of the United States- Richard Nixon. The letter was a detailed account of his life story from impoverished sharecropping, to serving his country in the army, to obtaining his degree through the G.I. Bill, and all in pursuit of the American dream. On the day of the court hearing, my grandparents arrived in court and were shocked

For Black Men/Ali Shakoor

to find a white attorney they had never seen before waiting for them. He identified himself as being from the United States District Court for the Southern District Court of Ohio and referenced that my grandfather's letter prompted a representative from the White House to contact his office. The lawyer proceeded to represent my grandparents at the hearing and convinced the mortgage company to accept the past due mortgage payments. My family's home was saved. This is the home where I was brought home to from the hospital, after my eighteen-year-old mother gave birth to me. This is the home where my extended family had laugh-filled holiday dinners and barbeques in the back yard. This is the home that is less than two miles from the cemetery where my grandfather was laid to rest. This is the home where my grandmother still lives to this day.

Home ownership is the most important commodity a person can have in this country. Why is this country so segregated in a way where there are poor black neighborhoods, known in unaffectionate fashion as ghettos, where the residents are generally only black and brown? It is intentional. Redlining is a policy that restricts lending opportunities for black families, while at the same time disinvests in areas within proximity to where black people reside. Up until post late 1960s civil rights legislation, there were blatant restrictive covenants in some communities, which precluded the sale of homes to prospective black buyers. In more recent times, racists are more limited in their ability to expressly deny blacks the most essential ingredient in the American pie; the opportunity for home ownership. Racists have to be more subtle nowadays.

Once it became illegal to put racist restrictions on paper, in black and white, bigoted white folks preceded to put their demeaning policies in practice through their patterns and actions. Blacks were often unable to secure bank loans in neighborhoods that were majority white. Predatory interest rates were offered to prospective black buyers. Of course, there was a lack of community investment from local governments. Most recently, in June of 2015, the United States Supreme Court issued a ruling in the case <u>Texas Department of Housing and Community Affairs v. Inclusive Communities Project</u> (2015), and held that policies that segregate minorities into poor neighborhoods need not reach the high hurdle of proving <u>intent</u>, when raising a claim that local policies violate the Fair Housing Act (FHA) of 1968. Instead, plaintiffs can produce evidence of lending, sales, leasing practices and zoning. The importance of this ruling lies in the fact that, people acting with racial animus are smart enough to conceal their efforts by avoiding the use of explicit racist language. Race relations have progressed in this country to the point where overt discriminatory practices are not only unlawful, but repugnant to the clear majority of American's regardless of race and ethnicity.

Disparate impact however is just as financially and psychologically devastating as being called "nigger" and seeing "whites only" signage. The racist is permitted to achieve his or her desired effect of denigrating your personhood, while smirking and shrugging their shoulders at your reaction. It can be infuriating. The effect of disparate impact-based discrimination creates a second-class citizenship for blacks. Recognize it and expose it for what it is. Just as racist people don't explicitly express racist views in company mixed with decent and evolved Americans, they similarly do not want the results of their actions to be exposed outside of their own vile subculture. Keep your cool, be vigilant, and expose it by protesting, writing and videotaping injustice. Make a record and spread the word with help from like-minded people.

Getting back to the topic of housing and why there are whole pockets of black poverty clustered around the country, I must direct you toward an article written for *The Atlantic*, called "The Case for Reparations," by Ta-Nehisi Coates as essential reading. The award winning and thoroughly researched piece details how blacks have been denied the right of home ownership in this country through practices like price hikes, deprivation and outright theft. These redlining tactics, along with joblessness and some other factors that are discussed in this book,
are the factors that produce violent ghettos and cause the incarceration rates that plague our people. Even today, our people are subjected to predatory lending practices and disparate treatment when trying to secure a bank loan to buy a home. Please read a recent February 28, 2019 *Washington Post* article titled "The Heartbreaking

For Black Men/Ali Shakoor

Decrease in Black Homeownership." It is infuriating to read but use the rage to fuel your resolve to advocate for justice and thrive toward owning a home.

Don't think for one second that the misery and emptiness that surrounds your crib is a reflection on your essence. You and those that you hold dear in your home and your neighborhood are destined to escape, if you wake up and stand up to find a way to flee out or figure out the tools improve your surroundings. That is why you are reading this book. The ghetto is not a prison. They just want you to think that way. There is nothing wrong with expressing pride in and representing your "hood," if you recognize that you are representing the best of your people - greatness and hope. You must know that you are better than what your government has forced upon you. The people, you, have the power to change oppressive factors in this society, just like our people have time and time again, since we arrived here in chains. The invisible chains that represent our attachment to poverty and inner-city decay can similarly be shed.

There was a period in America when we lived as black people free from the evils of crack cocaine. Sure, inner cities dealt with heroin abuse, and for those that could afford it, cocaine, but nothing compares to the crack epidemic that started in the early to mid- '80s, and just as industries were shutting down operations in cities all across the country. What a coincidence, huh? Crack cocaine is cheaply made, cheaply bought, extraordinarily addictive and has more to do with the destruction of our inner cities in the last 30 years than any other factor, coinciding with housing segregation and the outsourcing of employment opportunities. Your government was aware of the bourgeoning crack crisis and watched it explode. There are discrepancies about the depth of the government's involvement in allowing crack into our urban communities. Theories related to the Cold War era alliances in Central America that may have contributed to the sacrificing of poor black American humans, are controversial and beyond the scope of this book. But understand that middle- and upper-class white communities were not ravaged by crack addiction while their businesses were shuttered and became abandoned, but for the walking dead dope fiends who wasted away in them. These issues only happened in the urban black communities, and our government willfully allowed it to happen.

Your local governments chose not to allocate resources to invest in your communities being rebuilt. Instead, they invested in law enforcement to arrest addicts and dealers who took up crack dealing for what became the most viable means of earning a living. I often wonder what would have happened if my grandfather was unable to obtain a teaching position, and the Enterlake Iron and Toledo Shipbuilding Company shut down while crack cocaine moved in. Would he have turned to the crack trade to provide for his family? What if his hard work and determination was used for building a drug dealing empire, along with all the violence and criminal record that comes along with it? Instead of being the patriarch of a large family with five daughters who all either graduated from college and/or lived a healthy career-driven life with children of their own, he'd be a cliché for dismissive racists to shake their heads at.

If my grandfather had turned to drug dealing due to a lack of employment opportunities, he would have ended up dead or in prison. My mother and her sisters likely would have become addicts or criminals. I would be a third-generation product of government created chaos and systematic destruction. I'd be dead or in jail, or on my way there while caught up in the criminal justice system. I am lucky that my family, beginning with my grandparents, were fortunate enough to precede the government's racist crack influx/redlining/job outsourcing project by a generation or so. Lucky for me. There go I.

One way that the United States government decided to address the crack issue, was to declare a "war" against it, through a media facilitated campaign to show the drudgery and chaos that their crack plot had created. By exploiting the problem, it gave them a mandate to create a "nuclear option" of a law to incarcerate our people; the Anti-Drug Abuse Act of 1986. The language of this law shows that it was clearly designed to affect poor minorities and create a feeder system for mass incarceration with mandatory sentencing. This was most clearly demonstrated by the fact that the law mandated a minimum sentence of 5 years in prison without the possibility of parole for the possession of 5 grams of crack, while the law required 500 grams of powder cocaine for that same cruel and dispassionate sentence, based on the simple act of mere possession. That was a 100:1 disparity for what is basically the same drug. It was shameful and an intentional attack on the urban communities that took our people off the streets and out of the household, where they had a support system. They were denied the opportunity for rehabilitation in the community as the problem was often due to addiction.

If the possession was in the course of drug dealing, a five-year mandatory prison sentence would prevent the ability for better choices and redemption. Our people were prevented from staying close to one's support system and trying to become a productive member of the community. What the oppressive law did was provide free labor for an ever-growing prison industrial complex. By mandating prison, the laws condemned the individual to a dangerous and oppressive setting before sending them back out into a free society with a felony record and a likelihood of recidivism.

This country was awash with powder cocaine in the 1980s. People in the fields of entertainment, business, politics, and even parents in middle-class cul-de-sacs were using powder cocaine. It was everywhere. And this drug was expensive. Despite the ubiquity of powder cocaine in 1986, it still wasn't legal, obviously. It was also extremely dangerous and toxic for any unfortunate person who would accidently overdose or have a bad reaction. Considering the danger of the drug, you would think that the government, under predominantly majority white rule, headed by rightwing hero, Ronald Reagan, would do something about this issue with the same vigor as they did with crack cocaine. Why did Congress force a 100:1 disparity in sentencing, considering the dangers of power cocaine? It's because they made a calculated decision about whose freedoms, they determined to be expendable. White people in power saw their colleagues doing cocaine at parties and bathroom stalls of posh bars. It was looked upon as fashionable.

Crack, on the other hand was cheaper, crude and designed for poor people. Take out race and look upon wealth and privilege, and you'll recall the late Whitney Houston, a long-time cocaine user, infamously said, "Crack is whack," as she denied ever resorting to smoking on a crack pipe. She did not want that stigma associated with her. Crack was a street drug for poor people, mostly minority zombies headed toward prison or overdose. In 2010, under President Obama, Congress attempted to correct the evils caused by crack arrests and sentences at the federal level by passing the Fair Sentencing Act of 2010. The law did not go far enough, due to opposition from lobbyists in law enforcement and some conservatives in Congress, but it did reduce the sentencing disparity for 100:1 to 18:1 and it eliminated the 5-year mandatory minimum sentence for crack cocaine. This issue is not over, and there are still efforts being made to eliminate the sentencing disparity between crack and powder cocaine altogether, but so much damage has been done.

Nowadays, you see the opioid crisis being discussed in the media and being addressed at both the state and federal levels. There is concern and compassion for the users, regardless of the death and violence that comes along with it. Also, victims in the opioid crisis are usually white. The violence and decay typically occur in white areas. The government and media are discussing this issue as both a health crisis and societal tragedy, as opposed to pathology. It's infuriating. Where was such concern for our people? Where was the empathy and concern for black people?

The issues discussed in this chapter directly impact a problem, which is tagged with the all too familiar phrase "black-on-black crime." The phenomenon of black-on black-crime is an issue that has plagued our country. The policies that have ravaged urban communities have created an environment where criminality has run rampant. Random violent crimes are based on opportunity. Criminality related to drug dealing and gang activity is a product of where black people live, and government induced oppression which started shortly after the Civil War. Of course, blacks are more likely to offend against fellow blacks. Certain people, who are prone to crime, will offend against those in their own neighborhood. It is unfortunate, but it is based on common sense. Whites, similarly, offend against fellow whites.

I was disgusted when Rudy Giuliani took a shot against blacks on an episode of *Meet the Press* several years ago. It was during a segment about law enforcement's violent behavior toward the black community, and Rudy desired to bring up black-on-black crime as a distraction to deflect from the topic at hand. Giuliani proved that he doesn't care about the issue of police brutality targeted against blacks, and the lack of black representation in the police forces that patrol us, as he opined: *"White police officers wouldn't be in black neighborhoods, killing black men, if you weren't killing each other."* He continued, *"I find it very disappointing, that we are not discussing the fact that 93 percent of blacks are killed by other blacks...I would like to see the attention paid to that that you are paying to this."*

I personally find it pathetic that Rudy was unable to focus on the topic at hand. He deflected attention away from the conduct of those that he identifies with, to further victimize black people who are oppressed. I would like to see greater attention paid to the fact that Rudy is an aging, irrelevant political figure, who has developed a smug and nasty streak since he failed miserably at a presidential bid of which he assumed was his destiny. President Barack Hussein Obama sat in the Office that Rudy believed was his own personal entitlement, after he announced his run for the presidency over a decade ago. He'll spend the rest of his days moving further to the right in bitter fashion, and railing against anyone who looks like and shares the concerns of Barack Hussein Obama.

One of the more sickening aspects of Rudy's comments is the fact that he knows better. This wasn't some red state minded Joe sitting in his bedroom all bitter and leaving an ignorant comment on the topic in an online forum, with an opinion fortified by a mere high school education and daily escapism in rightwing talk radio. No, Rudy knows better. With his experience as a mayor, he knows specifically how local resources are allocated to the detriment of urban communities. He understands how redlining and zoning works to keep those of an ebony hue, in a perpetual cycle of urban poverty. As a former prosecutor, Rudy knows how the War on Drugs disparately impacts black men and creates a black market to do what the great rock poet, Ani DiFranco, would describe as "criminalize the symptoms, while you spread the disease."

Rudy knows better, but he felt compelled to take a chance on national television to deflect from the topic at hand, to protect the image of the often-sadistic American militarized police state. He was pathetic and thoroughly intellectually dishonest. Statistically speaking, according to a 2013 uniform crime report issued from the FBI, 90% of black victims are killed by fellow blacks. What Rudy did not mention, since it did not match up with his agenda of deflection, is the fact that 83% of white people in this country are killed by white offenders. Obviously, criminals tend to offend against those in which they share a community.

Whites also need to keep in mind that up until recent decades, and while my parents were growing up, whites took part in acts of violence and mayhem on innocent black people without ever being brought to justice. Many of these white people were working class, employed, and the heads of two-parent family units. Others who took parts in these acts of domestic terrorism on blacks were men in positions of power; police officers, politicians and businessmen. What was their excuse for committing acts of terror against black American citizens? In these instances, we're not discussing poverty and systematic oppression. We're talking pathological evil, by white men, and the white women who supported them, who simply wanted to feel superior and destroy fellow human beings. It's not that long ago. You can see their pictures in books and documentaries, as they didn't always hide under Klan sheets. Many of the white folks who committed these acts of terror are around the same age as Rudy. Now, they can sit back, and point and judge as white oppression has changed from systematic direct violent action, to systematic laws and policies. The common theme through all this diabolical conduct are the racists' feelings of superiority and the desire to maintain power.

Similarly, certain demographics like to belittle the Black Lives Matter movement, by accusing black people of ignoring or not focusing enough on blacks murdering one another. The Black Lives

For Black Men/Ali Shakoor

Matter movement is based on the fact that black victims are sometimes not validated as having worth, because the white assailant, often a police officer, may not be charged, let alone prosecuted. Police officers have unions and politically motivated officials who protect them. Whites, in general, are more likely to be given a benefit of the doubt; which is sickening. When certain demographics try to distract by bringing up black-on-black crime, to excuse whites who kill blacks and get away with it, they put forth a failing argument. When there is black-on-black crime, and they catch and prosecute the assailant, he/she is held accountable. There are thousands of black people in prison for committing crimes against fellow black people. There is accountability for the crimes; not excuses and cover up, such as when whites, particularly law enforcement, murder black people and the dignity of the victim and their families are invalidated. Black lives matter.

Black-on-black crime is an issue that black people have been aware of, because we are the ones directly impacted by it. I get so sick and tired of hearing from certain Al Sharpton and Jesse Jackson obsessed pundits disingenuously opining that "black leaders" are not addressing the black-on-black crime issue. This is a lie. At both the national level and locally, blacks that take on a leadership position have been pleading with the black community to stop offending against each other and to take better care of each other. President Obama discussed how black people need to take on better personal accountability, but of course, his critics, and those who do not legitimately care about the problem, perpetuate the lie that black people don't focus enough on black crime. We do focus on it and attempt to address it, while also acknowledging the oppressive factors that make it so hard to overcome. We have shown a tendency to hurt and destroy black skin, because it is something we have learned from our oppressors. Self-loathing, mixed with misplaced survival techniques, is an ongoing struggle that we are well to aware of, and will continue to fight to overcome.

My points in this chapter are about the fact that you must not think that your current environment or situation is the result of something solely controlled by internal or familial factors. You were born at a disadvantage caused by centuries of cruelty and oppression, and lingering coded words and prejudicial policies that will always make it harder for us. However, we've overcome so much in this great country. So many races and cultures in this country will always demand and strive for a nation based on peace, freedom and opportunity. Our people are headed in the right direction. This is a great time to be black in America. Of course, we have problems and still must remind America that #BlackLivesMatter. But think about how far we have come. At forty-four years old, I am part of the first post-Jim Crow generation. Recent times, but we have come far enough in this nation to have just finished a two-term presidency of a

For Black Men/Ali Shakoor

proud, self-identified black man named Barack Hussein Obama.

Let's keep growing. Do not stop learning and fighting for justice.

Chapter Three

Loving Our Country

After everything I've written so far, I still deeply love this country and so should you. There is more good than bad and we will continue to evolve as a positive work in progress. Our splendid first black president loves our people and he loves our country. He recently wrote a piece for the New York Times regarding voting rights—an issue I will address in a later chapter-- but this quote of his is absolutely on point: *"What makes our country great is not that we are perfect, but that with time, courage and effort, we can become more perfect. What makes America special is our capacity to change."* I considered making this the last chapter of the book, but by putting it here, with so much more to discuss and obstacles to strategically surpass, it is more honest and in line with President Obama's words, to discuss the greatness of America here. I have written about the oppression that we've had to overcome, and that which we still must endure, but to quote Kendrick Lamar, "We gon' be alright."

Do you ever watch movies set in the 1970s about our people, or listen to some of the music that originated during that time; the period before the horrors I described in the previous chapter? The '70s celebrated the previous decade's civil rights gains, by displaying

For Black Men/Ali Shakoor

an unapologetic reveling in blackness. Black is beautiful. As a man in my early forties, I can recall my family enjoying the black cultural experience of the 1970s in music, television, and film. I enjoyed it then, and I still adore looking back at that time in our history. Look at the afros and clothing! I enjoy the camaraderie in the way we addressed one another: "What's happening, blood?" Same ole, same as brother." "Stay black."

Blaxploitation movies depicted black leading characters doing badass shit, while getting over on the white man. Sure, the misogyny and glorification of criminality was nothing to look up to, but it was still beautiful to see black talent being able to showcase skills and charisma on the big screen. For decades, whites could depict anti-heroes and morally flawed protagonists. Why couldn't we have Superfly and Foxy Brown? Shaft gave us our own "Dirty Harry," and made Richard Roundtree a star, and allowed the late great Isaac Hayes to demonstrate his immense talents as a composer.

Musically, artists like Marvin Gaye and Curtis Mayfield continued to spread the word about the plight of our people. Stevie Wonder did the same, and he showed the world the true meaning of genius. Soul music, a fusion of the great black American creation that is rhythm and blues, along with our deep-rooted gospel tradition, continued its late 60s prime with Aretha Franklin and the Staple Singers uplifting our people. *"Respect Yourself,"* the Staple Singers implored. Damn right!

For Black Men/Ali Shakoor

Of course, I understand that there were still problems in our urban communities involving issues like drugs, prostitution and gang violence during the '70s. I know that we have victimized each other throughout history and the '70s was no exception. It just seems like love of blackness was more celebrated within our culture during that time. As we have just experienced the end of the legendary achievement of having a black family in the White House, now is a time to reaffirm the recognition of black excellence and beauty. That's my perception, based on the period in which I started to come of age. Different generations can reflect on different periods of black American exceptionalism.

My grandparents can look to the bravery we showed during World War II and the emergence of Jazz; a purely American tradition. The baby boomers generally excelled beyond the dreams of the previous generation and we have always proven to be successful culturally in sports and the arts. The civil rights movement showed our ability to weather oppressive conditions, strategize and force change. Through community organizing, exposure, voting and legislating, we strived to become more perfect, through our capacity to change.

Young people today can look toward black American exceptionalism with pride despite our struggles. There will always be struggles. And we will still thrive. We remain cultural icons to the extent that white musical artists continue to steal from our style and sound. Black beauty is personified along the spectrum from Beyoncé and Michael Ealy to Lupita Nyong'o and Idris Elba. Our people have always excelled in entertainment, and the bean counting of award show nominations does not reduce the impact of performances that create financial wealth for the artist and stirs the souls of those of us inspired by their talent. Moguls like Oprah Winfrey and Tyler Perry mentor and employ our people. They change lives through charity. They serve as role models for others to follow their example. They remind us that we are capable of greatness.

Floyd Mayweather just retired as the best boxer of his generation. We can only hope that his abusive ways have ended, and he will spend his retirement becoming a champion outside of ring by atoning for his past and seizing the opportunity for redemption. Lebron and Serena are each the best of their era in basketball and tennis, respectively. Serena came straight out of Compton with her sister Venus to show that anything is possible in this country. Lebron James lived in poverty in Akron, Ohio with a single mother; a cliché. Yet, he not only took advantage of his athletic gifts to become a legend, he is a wonderful man; married to the mother of his children, never arrested and charitable. Importantly, Lebron is also activist minded and he cares greatly about the plight of our people. His mindset is in the mold of brave and militant black athletes from the 60s like Muhammad Ali, Bill Russell, Kareem Abdul-Jabbar and Jim Brown. The hateful and jealous can ridicule his decisions to make life moves in the best interest of himself and his family or mock him for not winning "enough" championships. It does not matter. LeBron James is and will always be an example of overcoming an impoverished broken home, avoiding a statistical probability, and establishing himself as a splendid and accomplished black American man.

Black American icons like Beyoncé and Kendrick Lamar are unafraid to speak truth to power about racial injustice and the importance of black pride. These are compelling times. Read and listen to their words. The Obama presidency has reinvigorated leaders amongst our people. He has instilled us with pride and has triggered a hunger to accelerate paths toward economic and political equality.

This country produced Prince Rogers Nelson, aka, Prince. We lost him at 57 years old in a tragic health and addiction related accident that shocked the world. Literally, the world grieved. Prince is arguably the most talented recording artist in music history. The word "genius" gets thrown around a great deal in society, but Prince was unquestionably a genius. He was a gifted singer, songwriter and dancer. Musicianship is where Prince's genius truly shined. The brother would compose and produce albums all by himself, while playing every single instrument. Think about that. If you want to see a display of black excellence, spend some time watching the last 30 minutes of the movie Purple Rain as Prince owned the stage with an unparalleled display of talent. And, if you want to bear witness to a more recent show of black excellence, look up Prince's solo during the George Harrison tribute at the Rock and Roll Hall of Fame concert in 2004. Prince was on stage with several prominent rock musicians, all of them white, during the performance of "While My Guitar Gently Weeps." When it was his turn to play a guitar solo, one of the most memorable and bold performances in rock history took place. Prince proceeded to slay. He enhanced what had been a rather banal group performance while fitting along with the song, but he also improvised something that is not describable with words. You must see it and listen to it. It was remarkable. At the end of the song, Prince tossed the guitar in the air—you never see it land—and then proceeded to walk off stage, strutting like a real jive soul brotha. Please put this book down and go watch the performance.

In the last years of Prince's life, he prominently supported black causes, and particularly, helped expose the horrors of police brutality against our people. He wrote a song in support of Freddie Gray and the protestors in Baltimore. At the Grammys in 2015 and proudly supporting the afro hair style in his later years, Prince boldly told the audience and millions watching at home: "Albums still matter. Like books and *black lives*, albums still matter." That's how our splendid Prince chose to close out the 2015 Grammy ceremonies to introduce Album of the Year, after patiently waiting for the conclusion of the theater audience's lauding and long-standing ovation. Prince was a proud black American and a representation of the best of what our race and country has produced for the world of music.

As I write these words, the world is also mourning the loss of Muhammad Ali. Less than two months after the loss of our genius, Prince, the most talented recording artist who ever lived, we lost, arguably, the most famous and impactful man who ever lived. Muhammad Ali represents the epitome of American values: religious freedom, respect for constitutional rights, both moral and physical courage. As a black man, he's everything for me and I'll always carry his inspiration. I also proudly wear his name. As a small child, my family went through a brief Muslim phase; which was common among many young politically conscious black folks in the '70s. I think I was roughly four or five years old and given the option of choosing my first name. I chose the name Ali, because even though his career was essentially over, the residue of his near two-decade cultural impact still intoxicated our people. He was seemingly always on television and in magazines. My proud black family always spoke of him, and I would often see clips of the earlier Ali on sports and news programs. I was born and bred into a world where Muhammad Ali was the most significant black icon alive.

As I got older, I began to read and study more about Ali. Along with Malcolm X, Muhammad Ali was a key force in my development. I was taught about the beauty and dignity of our people, in continuous conflict with a rigged evil system perpetrated by the white race. Calling him a personal hero, does not really do my thoughts the proper expression. Outside of my family, no person has had as much of an influence on my worldview and personality as the great Muhammad Ali. Ali preached strength and defiance, but more importantly, he demonstrated those attributes in how he lived his life.

I have read more biographies about Muhammad Ali growing up, than I have about any other historical figure. There was never enough or too much information to retain about such an extraordinary human being. He was a proud black man. He was flawed like any human, but he was the embodiment of black strength. No disrespect to men like Joe Louis and Jesse Owens, and I understand that they were in an earlier, less free, time, but I understand and relate to the rage and fight of Ali, more than characteristics like quiet strength and so-called respectability. Ali demanded to be treated equal, rather than ask or hope for it. Like Malcolm X, Ali joined the Nation of Islam. He was seduced by their tenants of the white man being a representation of the devil himself and our people being superior. Also, like Malcolm X, Ali eventually discovered the true nature of Islam, and he decided to live a life based on equality for all and peace.

Muhammad Ali was a man who decided to be extraordinary. He grew up a black boy in Jim Crow enforced Louisville, Kentucky. He could have lived a meaningless life or perhaps a decent and nondescript life. No, Muhammad Ali took advantage of his natural athletic gifts and got the most out of himself. He excelled as an amateur boxer to such an extent that he was selected to represent our country at the 1960 Olympic Games in Rome, Italy. Muhammad Ali, our splendid black man, proved to be the best amateur light heavyweight in the world, by winning the gold medal.

As a professional, along with his athletic gifts, Ali used his charisma and quick wit to market himself into a young star. Of course, he backed it up in the boxing ring by demonstrating hand speed and swift feet, and with unparalleled reflexes. Put this book down for a few minutes and look on YouTube at prime Ali fighting between 1964 and 1967. No heavyweight before or since looked like that. We'll never know what other amazing feats could have occurred during that prime, because Ali made the most profound and important career decision of any athlete or celebrity in history. He took on the United States government as a plaintiff. They tried and convicted Ali for refusing an induction into the draft for the Vietnam War. Muhammad Ali was facing five years in prison. He also lost out on millions of dollars in income and more prime years of his athletic career. He dealt with scorn and death threats. Yet, he had the strength of character to stand by his convictions as a conscientious objector to the war based on his religious beliefs. In 1971, after many folks in the nation, of all races, began to admire and lionize Ali for being correct in opposing the war, while also recognizing his sacrifices, the

Supreme Court of the United States of America ruled in Muhammad Ali's favor. A black man took on Uncle Sam, the system, and won.

You probably know a lot about Ali's return to the ring, and the battles with Joe Frazier, and his legendary conquering of Foreman in Zaire, Africa, among other battles in the greatest heavyweight era in boxing history throughout the '70s. But also understand that Ali never stopped preaching about and exemplifying black excellence. He always spoke truth to power. Ali also was loyal and charitable to people of all colors and ethnicities around the world.

After Ali retired and grew sick with Parkinson's disease, he slowed and lost his ability to speak, but he never stopped giving of himself. He gave money and time. Ali traveled abroad to help free hostages. He had the courage to light the flame at the opening ceremonies of 1996 Olympics, while the disease caused him to shake uncontrollably before the crowd and millions watching at home. Ali gave of himself completely until his body gave out at the age of seventy-four on June 3, 2016. That night, ESPN and several news networks openly mourned and eulogized him until dawn; many reporters and pundits got out of bed, respectfully dressed in suits, and drove to the studio to speak about "The Greatest." Our black man, a representative of our people, was mourned worldwide for over a week leading up to his funeral which was televised live on numerous networks for the world to see. And people from all over the world flew into Louisville, Kentucky to say goodbye to this man and touch the hearse. Many were sobbing and tossing flowers as the procession rolled down his hometown streets. Those streets gave birth to a black, Muslim American, man, who represented the best of not only our race, or our country, but of humanity. Muhammad Ali is one of the few most compelling and significant human beings who have ever breathed air on this planet. He is special, and he is our people. He's an American hero.

In science, Neil deGrasse Tyson helps explain how our planet works and inspires young black children to explore. I took my mother to an appointment for a colonoscopy in June of 2016 and was delighted to see the doctor who handled the procedure. He was teenage looking, bow tie wearing brother in his twenties. We are underrepresented in the science and math fields. This is not due to lack of acumen, but rather, what's lacking is opportunity and focus. Our people have always demonstrated the ability to excel. In this country, any career is possible. Make sure to remember that. Make sure to take advantage of the opportunity and be prepared to proudly trample over barriers and ignore haters along the way. Follow the examples set for you. Don't stop until you accomplish your goals.

I was recently at a community gathering where there was a panel discussion about racist police practices that target young black males. There were probably close to a hundred people in the small community center who sat for several hours listening to small groups of discussions about how best to address the problem. Predictably, political opinions and temperament ran the gamut from the need for violent revolution, to the political and pragmatic approach. I was dismayed to hear some local leaders consistently rant about the evil nature of our country. The typical complaints of "stolen people on a stolen land" rhetoric was bantered about. Of course, that is true, but what is the point of generalizing our country as something wicked, while ignoring what is and has been good and noble. Every civilization since the beginning of time has committed atrocities and horrific policies that needed to be eradicated, and later looked back upon with shame and disgust. Everywhere, even "Mother Africa." Even "Mother Africa" prior to oppressive European colonization, had elements of evil oppression and violence in most every nation. It is patently intellectually dishonest to think or speak as if only white Americans, or only that only those of European descent have practiced slavery, sexism, oppression, and evil. It is about the nature of man, and the need to continue to demand that we as humans strive to do better.

I can only shake my head ruefully when I hear some militant minded blacks rant about "stolen people on a stolen land" and how the very essence of our country is evil and racist. Yet, they are quick to praise Jesus and their Christian faith. There's a disconnect with such a thought process. Our people in "Mother Africa" were practicing different types of faiths and belief systems long before the birth of Christ. What we do know, is that the United States was founded with the Christian faith as the dominant religion. The Christian God is referenced in our Pledge of Allegiance. It is referenced on our money. Plantation owners would beat, own, and plunder our people while worshipping in the Christian faith, like how those whites who benefitted from the oppression of Jim Crow would think nothing of going to a church and singing hymns after watching the lynching of our people. White racists have always found justification for their racist belief system in the Christian Bible. Hell, the Ku Klux Klan has a strong Christian faith as part of their ideological foundation. It is nonsensical, in so many ways, to hate this country, and hate white people, but love Jesus. That does not mean that I have a problem with Christianity or think that our people should not believe in such a faith. I do not have a problem with any religious person who practices any religion, that gives them peace and strength, and does not oppress the rights and beliefs of those who do not practice or believe the same. I just have a problem with intellectual dishonesty and hypocrisy.

This great country allows for freedom to practice the religion of one's choosing, if practiced lawfully. We have a true mix of all types of different religions in this country, coexisting peacefully. There is no prevalent religious based violence in our streets, let alone generational genocide like in other parts of the world. Despite the "Judeo-Christian values" we hear so much about regarding the dominant religion in this country, we should remain constantly reminded that this country was founded upon freedom of religion and freedom from religion, if one so chooses.

One of my personal heroes is Malcolm X. Growing up, I remember always seeing this large hard cover book around our home. It had red, black and white letters and an intense looking bespectacled gentleman on the cover. As a child, I never thought of reading it. My reading consisted of whatever was assigned in elementary school. On my free time, I was obsessed, just as I obviously still am, with sports and pop culture. I read a lot of biographies and magazines growing up about my sports and entertainment heroes.

During my freshman year of high school, I got into some trouble, and wound up sentenced to a few days of in-school suspension. I cannot specifically recall what I was punished for, but I think it was for punching a dude in the gym, or "promoting" two other kids to fight each other after school. I threw more punches between sixth and tenth grade, than all other periods of my life combined together. It was a difficult time for me, personally. I decided to spend my time on suspension by reading The Autobiography of Malcolm X.

Problems at home involving a wicked stepfather who was abusive toward my mother and sister were weighing more and more on my psyche. My mother had left him by then, but the mental trauma remained. Also, being black in America obviously brings on a host of challenges. Mom always made sure my sister and I were in quality, meaning white, school districts that had good academic reputations. Worthington was one of the more "quality" school districts in the Columbus, Ohio area during the 1980s. My racial identity was something that I was more aware of in my preteen period. Not my obvious blackness, which I always carried with pride, but the realization that I was one of few blacks in a vastly majority white school district. My best friend to this day, Chris, was my closest buddy and black, but I had my fair share of white friends as well.

Even though I never experienced any visceral injustice beyond the occasional taunt of 'nigger' or 'blackie' throughout my childhood, by the time I was two years into the move to suburban Worthington, Ohio even that was rare. My high school wasn't like some dramatic movie, filled with bullies and open bigotry. There was racial harmony, generally. Still, being one of very few blacks, always made you stand out and feel like a bit of an outsider. I was athletic, smart and well liked, but there were still too many "can I feel your hair?" type moments and jokes at my people's expense that led to my feeling like Malcolm's chapter about being a "mascot." I had reached the point in my life where I wanted to read and explore this man that I knew very little about. To this day, it's the best and most important book I have ever read.

For Black Men/Ali Shakoor

Malcolm, like this great country, had the courage and humility to evolve and show a capacity to change. What I respect most about Malcolm, our outstanding black American man, was his ability for self-reflection and analysis. As Malcolm reached adulthood, he refused to live his life as a "mascot" for the white race, while our people suffered, so his disillusionment turned into a life of crime. Then while incarcerated, he had the personal will to better himself by reading, understanding, and deciding that he would better himself and his race, as opposed to leading a dead-end life of crime. Malcolm X sought solutions to address the racism in this country. After leaving prison, he found guidance in the Nation of Islam (NOI), where there were other angry black folks looking to claim a sense of self-determination to overcome oppression. Unfortunately, this sect had a twisted version of Islam based on hatred of whites. The NOI would tap into the justified fury and frustration of young blacks and blend a distorted mixture of Islamic tenets along with legitimately useful plans for empowerment and black success. Later in life, through experience, Malcolm X learned to accept the fulfilling and beautiful relationship with mankind and Islam, while disregarding the hatred, hypocrisy, and corruption that tainted the Nation of Islam. His insistence on defeating oppression and elevating the black race did not wane, just his perspective, as he evolved to become the best that he could be. Malcolm X was one of our greatest of Americans and a great example for life, growth, reflection and change.

For Black Men/Ali Shakoor

As I write this book, we are just past the forty-year anniversary of the Dr. Martin Luther King Jr. led March from Selma to Montgomery in support of voting rights in Alabama. I will most certainly discuss the importance of voting later in this book. Dr. King fully understood voting as a crucial right for Americans to experience. His leadership helped to insure the passage of the Voting Rights Act of 1965. Dr. King literally dedicated his life to making this country a better place. He led, but he obviously did not do it alone. Our people have not and do not fight for civil rights alone. For the past 100 years, we have never made up more than our current 12-13 percent of the U.S. population. One of the reasons why this country is so great, is because of the assistance and leadership of those who do not look like us, who have aided us in trying to overcome oppression.

Many, though not nearly enough, white Americans, since the time we were brought here, have advocated for our people. Some tried to peacefully change thoughts and laws, while others, like John Brown tried to encourage a violent revolution. Point being, we would not be where we are now, as far as ending slavery, and on through more recent civil rights gains, without the sacrifices of many woke white folks. The freedom riders included many whites who traveled to the deep and oppressive south, to help register black people to vote and take part in peaceful protests. Many were beaten, some were murdered, but they tried to make this a better nation for us all.

40 years after Selma, it is important to really appreciate the brilliance of what Dr. King did for this country. As a younger man, I admired him, but foolishly felt that his methods were too soft and patient. I found it asinine to put up with water hoses and spit from whites, with or without badges. We should have taken part in an armed revolution, I once believed. That was naiveté on my part, and I still see it from some radical-minded blacks today in how they view Dr. King and his ideology. You cannot fight evil with force, when you are outnumbered and outgunned. That's a nihilistic quest for suicide. What Dr. King encouraged, and something I have found to be effective whenever I have experienced oppressive injustice, is exposure.

Almost ten years ago, my family experienced a great deal of injustice during my sister's divorce proceedings. The plaintiff's account, which can be found online, explains: My former brother-in-law, troubled about the divorce at the time and carrying personal demons, began to act out his resentment on my then four-year-old niece. He suddenly, for the first time in her life, and by his own admission in writing, began to take her in the shower with him when she was four- both completely nude. There were also allegations about perverse unwanted touching when he had her in his custody; all the while mocking my family about the abuse we overcame at the hands of my stepfather.

For Black Men/Ali Shakoor

Considering what my family had experienced with my sister being a survivor of sexual abuse herself, the situation involving my niece proved to be the most trying period of my life. My former brother-in-law is white, a lawyer, and came from a somewhat wealthy family. My sister was unable to find quality legal representation, due to the politics of how her ex-husband's actions could negatively impact his legal career, and how it would impact the reputation of the courthouse that employed him as an assistant juvenile public defender. An expert in the field privately advised my sister to get counseling and accept the fact that some child molesters in society have the clout to get away with it, and she could risk losing custody if she pressed too hard for justice. Unacceptable.

All the family law court justices recused themselves from sitting on the case, except one judge. Although this particular judge held the title of a "visiting judge," that was a title in name only. The judge on my sister's case sat on the bench longer than the judges who recused themselves. She retired, but never left the bench. The same concerns about bias and impropriety that applied to the judges that recused themselves, applied to her even more. There is too much about the case to discuss here, but a great deal of information can be found online. I have practiced law in areas of Florida in major metropolitan cities that would be considered "the South" in location only, and I've practiced in courthouses in Florida that resemble something like *To Kill a Mockingbird* and visually appear to represent everything you could imagine about the small towns in the "Deep South." Yet, I have never in my life experienced or even witnessed such blatant, in your face, injustice, like I experienced in Franklin County, Columbus, Ohio. Frankly, I was in a perpetual hate-filled rage, as I took on the case to represent my sister in Ohio and help my dear niece. It was infuriating and mentally trying. I lost my cool in anger and bewilderment on several occasions, and eventually, my conduct caused me to receive sanctions from the Florida Bar where I am admitted to practice.

I do not regret helping my family as an uncle/brother, but as an attorney, I do regret losing my calm and cool; something I'll caution other young black men about in later chapters. However, my point here is that what turned my sister's case around was exposure; particularly exposure to other white people. My family was experiencing something similar to the many victims of the Catholic Church scandal or Penn State's Jerry Sandusky, in the vain of no accountability and containment, through the use of power and privilege. Children are in danger in certain churches, school districts, detention centers and courthouses all over the country. Well, my family decided to make as many people as possible aware of what was going on in my sister's case. Exposure is what turned my sister's case around and produced a quick settlement. Exposure is what ultimately kept my niece safe, after any problematic conduct by my niece's father resulted in material being sent to his place of employment and all over the internet. If the legal system wouldn't hold him accountable and make him stop, the next best method was shame and embarrassment. Most people are good, fair-minded, humans who want justice and equal protection under the law. Such people condemn injustice. You'll find in the legal profession, those who are acting wickedly and unethically will desire empty courtrooms, off the record conversations, and good ole "circle the wagons." When you encounter injustice, open the doors and turn on the lights for all to see.

Most white people are fair and good, because most people are fair and good. Dr. King understood the importance of showing other parts of the country what was going on under Jim Crow. Most white people were appalled to see what fellow white Americans were doing, once the media would spread the footage of beatings, and the reports of bombings and lynching. Most fair-minded Americans decided that such conduct was patently unacceptable in this country. The civil rights legislation of the 1960s never would have happen if the evolved standards of decency in this country were not instilled in most white Americans. Even through anger and despair, trust the good people in your community, and in our country to choose the side of fairness and justice.

The other key to exposure is the law. Yes, the same country's laws that once justified our enslavement, and still today impact us in negative disparate fashion, yet still, created the template for reform.

For Black Men/Ali Shakoor

The Constitution applies to our people even though most of the racists who founded this country barely considered us to be human. The system of government that was created, allowed for changes to create a path toward equality. In a representative democracy, the will of good people can come to pass. The same government that wickedly denied our right to exist as free men was forced to help end the Civil War by granting our people freedom from slavery, via the Thirteenth Amendment. Shortly thereafter, the Fourteenth Amendment was passed to insure our rights as citizens. The Fifteenth Amendment then provided for the right to vote.

Of course, a racist element remained in this country which tried to minimize the gains of the "Civil War Amendments." Many white people did not want to give up power, or worse, just had a deep-rooted hatred of our people because of our very existence. All over the country, but particularly in the South, there was pushback known as "black codes" and later, Jim Crow. Even today certain demographics like to perpetuate their own privilege or are just fueled by racism, but obviously, it was worse back then. Due to exposure, blatant overt racism was becoming socially unacceptable enough to the extent that it was difficult to justify a second-class citizenship for blacks. The term *separate but equal* had to incorporate the term *equal* to at least put forth the appearance of constitutionality. The foundation of law-abiding society where all men are deemed to have been created equal, caused racists in positions of power to start using the coded language and dog-whistling tactics which are less prevalent but still exist today. This is the power of the law and the importance of taking advantage of our means for enforcement.

An era of legislative civil rights advancement occurred in the late 1960s, under the Johnson administration. Fueled by the power of Dr. King's advocacy, this nation was forced to make further efforts in the advancement of our constitutional rights. Following the momentum of the <u>Brown v. Board of Education</u> (1954) decision, which was the landmark case that established the law, that *"separate but equal"* was inherently unconstitutional, Congress under the Lyndon Johnson administration was mandated to effectuate further change. By creatively finding authority under the Commerce Clause in the United State Constitution, the Civil Rights Act of 1964 was passed in part, to ensure that individual states, particularly in the South, could no longer allow businesses open to the public to discriminate against our people.

Shortly thereafter, the Voting Rights Act of 1965, further insured our right to vote, as guaranteed by the Fifteenth Amendment to the United States Constitution. No longer, were whites permitted to impose barriers to the right to vote, such as "literacy tests" and "poll taxes." If you have not already, please see the movie *Selma* and engage in independent research about how Dr. King had the courage and strategic acumen to gather a peaceful, nonviolent *army*, in a movement to shame the White House and Congress into providing the essential black American right of suffrage. Even though the Supreme Court has recently attempted to water down this law, the effect of it is strong enough to protect our rights to vote; notwithstanding disenfranchisement via felony convictions and other obstacles, which will be discussed in a later chapter. These civil rights era laws of the late 1960s have been further modified and litigated throughout the decades since. They never have been and never will be completely overturned. Being forty-four years old, as I've stated, I am a member of the first post-Jim Crow generation of black Americans. See, it was not that long ago at all. We have come a long way and our country will continue to improve the lives of our people.

Another issue to keep in mind as an America citizen is the fact that we must recognize that we are amid a perpetual global war on terror against radicalized Islamic fundamentalists. There are evil terroristic people all around the world, and most frighteningly, right here at home in the USA, who aim to murder us for our very way of life. They hate us for our very existence, and this is based on their twisted manipulation of the Muslim faith.

On September 11, 2001 I was in law school and living in Columbus, Ohio. I was in my second year and worked as a teaching assistant (TA) for Property Law. I woke up on that September morning a bit tired and feeling the residue from the Sade concert my girlfriend and I went to the night before. I often stayed at my then girlfriend's apartment, which she shared with her three children. My day was fairly light until my evening TA session.

I was never one to enjoy getting out of bed, but my girlfriend told me to wake up because there was something going on involving the World Trade Center (WTC). I didn't think much of it. When she mentioned a plane hitting a tower at the WTC, I just did not see the big deal. Not too much longer afterwards, she returned to the bedroom and mentioned that another tower had been hit, and there was talk of a terror attack. My groggy mind searched for thoughts formulated around what happen the last time terrorists tried to bomb the WTC in 1993; the specifics of which I simply could not recall at that moment, but it did not seem like something to rouse myself out of bed over. About thirty minutes later she came back voiced with a mix of concern and confusion to tell me that a third plane had crashed into the Pentagon. I started to come to the realization that a life-changing tragedy was happening.

I spent the next several hours glued to the television in a state of shock. This was an attack on my country and my fellow Americans were murdered, while the rest of us suffered in grief. By the time I made my way to the class I was tutoring for the evening session, one could feel the sense of anxiety and gloom we all shared together. After a truncated session, I made my way back to my girlfriend's apartment and picked up a bottle of liquor to guide us through a night of news programs and grief. It was a profoundly sad night. Over and over, we watched the images of the two towers crumbling to the ground. Human bodies fell from the sky. While the liquor mixed with my understanding of American political history, I slurred how important of an event this was in our lives. I knew our nation would soon be at war. I knew we were living through a monumentally important moment in what would inevitably become a key point in American history.

The next morning, we groggily walked my lady's nine-year-old daughter to the bus stop, which was after a nap of sleep in the wee hours of the morning. This was the first time I had ever joined the young girl on the walk to the bus stop. I believe she usually walked with other children from the building. This time my girlfriend and I walked with her. Once we got to the bus stop there was an adult with every child in sight. Apparently, this was a first. The babies were hugged tight before they boarded the bus. They were taking a journey to school unlike any other they had ever experienced. Their country was about to encounter something they'd never known before in their short lives- War.

After the bus left, and while on the way to a local diner for breakfast, my lady and I went to pick up an aptly named USA Today. We were hungover and in a state of mourning. At the bottom of the front page of the paper, I read eyewitness accounts about the horror of 9/11. People spoke of what they saw and how they felt searching for family and friends. Some people tried to flee from the city on crowded roads and highways. The words on the paper became blurry and for the first time in a long time in my adult life, I began sobbing.

This War on Terror continues. There are men and women all over the world and most importantly, right here at home, who want to kill us Americans. They have a twisted viewpoint of Islam and a rage about some of our oppressive misconduct in the Middle East. These terrorists do not make a differentiation between black Americans and white Americans. They hate us for who we are and what we represent. They do not believe in freedom and equality for all. They do not believe in equal rights for women or for those in the LGBT community. These terrorists hate you and want to destroy all of us. They want to destroy America.

This is not just about radical Islam, either. Russia has been our main global adversary since the end of WWII and waged a cyber war here in the 2016 presidential election in support of Donald Trump and a desire to mock American democracy. North Korea is designing nuclear bombs that can reach our land and its government promulgates anti-American rhetoric in their society. However, right now a major threat to our great country is radicalized white nationalism. White nationalism is really a global phenomenon, spreading throughout Europe and also demonstrated by the recent scumbag who slaughtered praying Muslims at a mosque in New Zealand. White nationalism is based on a belief in white supremacy, ethnic cleansing and of course, maintaining control. In our country, too many white men, motivated by the "Make American Great Again" rhetoric, still bitter about the Obama presidency, and concerned about so many black and brown faces, will attempt their vile acts of terror on innocent citizens. There was a surge in white nationalist activity during the Obama presidency, and now, under Trump, they feel emboldened.

So many of our people have fought, been maimed, and died, while defending this great country from enemies foreign and domestic, and this is since the establishment of these United States. Even while fighting evil white racists and the cowards who abet them, our people have still understood the importance of American principals. We have just known and demanded that such principals also apply to us. I am sure that every one of you has relatives who have served this country. Remember to think of them on Veterans Day and Memorial Day and whenever you hear our National Anthem. Always be proud to be an American. Even if you choose to sit out the Anthem as an act of protest to institutional racism, you should still be proud of being an American. There is nothing more American than protests for equality and fighting for freedom.

On a lighter and still relevant note, what sports teams do you root for? Do you rant about and feel hatred for this country about what they've done to us, but still represent and love your favorite squad? This is another disconnect. It is emotionally dishonest. Love your country for all the reasons I mentioned, but also love it like you love your team. Every institution and business in this country is a product of a racist past; including the teams your root for.

Pro basketball is my favorite team sport, and right now I root for the Los Angeles Lakers because of Ohio native, Lebron James. When it comes to football, I have rooted for the Oakland Raiders since I was about nine years old. On January 22, 1984, I was at a Super Bowl party with my family. I had been a sports fan all my short life up to that point, but had followed players more than teams. I rooted for Dr. J. and Walter Payton and a few other stars that were prominent in the media at the time.

But when Marcus Allen made his famous reverse of field and legendary 74-yard run, I was in love. I had a new favorite player, so his team became my team. My dedication to the Raiders was sealed a few years later, when I got around to reading another book that I had always seen around the family home; *They Call Me Assassin*, the autobiography of the great Jack Tatum. It was such a great read. I was seduced by the characters and lore of the Raiders. Tatum also played for the Ohio State Buckeyes while in college. Though college sports were pretty much an afterthought for me at that time in my life, I understood that Ohio State meant something important. Yes, I understand that the city of Oakland was and is oppressive to poor black people, and the Black Panthers initially thrived there, but I am not going to stop loving the Oakland Raiders, who are soon to be called the Las Vegas Raiders. I am not going to deny myself this joy.

My love for The Ohio State University is absolute. I graduated from there in 1996 at the legendary "Horseshoe." My mother graduated from there before me, and my sister, after me. I always followed and supported them over the years, but only to a certain extent. Because I had always been more of a pro sports head, I am embarrassed to say, I did not even attend a home game while I went there for undergrad, between '93- '96. I rooted for them, but I was busy rushing to obtain my BA degree in two years and nine months, dating, and just trying to figure out life as a young black man. My sports obsessions were saved for the NBA, boxing, and my Raiders. For some reason, my love affair and sense of ownership for Ohio State really manifested itself post-college. In my 20s, while trying to maintain and make it in life, I reached the point where the Buckeyes became extremely important to me. I graduated there, as the first grandchild in my large extended family with a college degree. The school represented me, and me, them. I took an emotional stake in our football and basketball teams. At the beginning of my final year in Columbus, Ohio, I felt nerves and elation during the final moments when we won the first football national championship of my lifetime on January 3, 2003.

I brought my love for Ohio State with me to my life here in Tampa, Florida. It is a major part of my identity. I walk the streets wearing various sorts of Buckeye gear. My "flag," I call it.

Particularly down here in Florida, I proudly represent my Midwest school. I damn near had a stroke when we lost to Vince Young's Texas Longhorns in 2005. I argued and apologized for my school when the Florida Gators bullied us in both football and basketball in 2006 and 2007, respectively. I eventually moved into an apartment within walking distance of a Buckeye alumni bar, where I led us all in standing on the patio for the National Anthem, before I emotionally cheered as we won the second football national championship of my lifetime in 2015. I am an Ohio State Buckeye, born and bred. I love them like family.

Does Ohio State have a history of racism and oppression against blacks? Of course, it does. It is part of America. But this university also produced Jesse Owens, who stood up for American values and black excellence, while embarrassing Hitler at the 1936 Olympics. The university birthed out me and my immediate family, who are fine people and fighters for justice. Hell, despite the horrible injustice my family experienced in the court systems of Columbus, Ohio, I still love my city.

The point I am making in concluding this chapter, is that you all have a team, or school, or neighborhood, or city, which you claim and love. You do not let the fact that such entities are affected by, endorsed, or participated in racial oppression against our people, cheat you out of that love. In that same sense, do not allow the racist

For Black Men/Ali Shakoor

aspects of this country cheat you, or stop you from loving America. Take ownership. Participate. Respect and cherish our place in this great country, as you can help improve our capacity to change for the better. Systematic racism is contrary to the laws and foundation of our Constitution and in direct conflict to the values that we as a nation stand for. Therefore, we have successfully been able to use the law, along with the commitment from American people who demand justice and equality under the law. Oppressive white supremacy is a worldwide phenomenon. Not to mention, you will find injustice and discrimination against certain demographics in many countries governed by people of color. Imagine being a homosexual in Nigeria or Jamaica, for example. There is no Utopia to escape to in the world, where there is not some form of economic and racial/ethnic oppression. Our people have helped make this country a world leader throughout history. This land is our land, too. Take pride and ownership, as we strive to improve our lives and communities.

Chapter Four

<u>Becoming Politically Active</u>

2016 was the most bizarre and surreal political election of my lifetime. Countless books will be written, and movies made, about Donald J. Trump's seemingly impossible run toward the White House. Trump seized on the anger and resentments from certain demographics to propel him toward the Republican nomination and then the presidency of the United States. I felt physically sick on the night of November 8, 2016 as the man was elected into the White House. At the time, Trump becoming president felt like the most catastrophic event to happen to this country since 9/11.

These are emotional and important times. Certain demographics that support Trump are angry about the way the country has changed, providing more opportunities for black and brown people. They just experienced eight years of a self-identified black president named Barack Hussein Obama. Under President Obama, though our economy had greatly improved since the debacle of the George W. Bush years, and our country was kept safe from a large 9/11 scale attack, and we deescalated from fighting two simultaneous ground wars in the Middle East, and gas prices were right around $2.00 a

For Black Men/Ali Shakoor

gallon when President Obama was leaving office, certain demographics remained bitter and resentful. I am very proud of President Obama. I am proud that he is unapologetic about his love for black culture. I am proud of his great accomplishments and grace under fire. I miss class and integrity in the White House. I really miss the Obama family.

Certain demographics despised eight years of the Obama administration. Of course, not all of it is about race. Some of these people are simply partisan or extremely conservative by nature. They would be resentful and bent out of shape, regardless of what a Democrat president accomplished while in office because of policy differences. Also, my life and finances improved during Obama's eight years, and I am sure millions of others would say the same. But in fairness, some folks were experiencing joblessness or other financial difficulties. They may have harbored a good faith belief that their dire straits were related to the Obama years.

Never forget, some folks voted for Obama twice and switched to Trump in 2016. Some just didn't like or trust Hillary Clinton. Many have buyer's remorse, in light of what has happen in our government since the 2016 election. But plenty of social conservatives who would like to see abortion outlawed and gay marriage laws repealed, are impassioned by the desire to see an alleged conservative Christian win the White House.

The point is there are numerous reasons why people care about national politics. I will discuss the importance of more localized politics later. It is just so crucial that you stay engaged because others are focused, and they are voting on issues that directly affect you. One of the most important duties of the president is the appointment of federal judges. The highest level of federal judgeship is the United States Supreme Court (USSC). The reason why homosexuals were recently granted the right to marry is because of a 2015 USSC opinion. A USSC opinion in 1954 declared the law of "separate but equal" unconstitutional, which mandated that states could no longer require people of different races to go to separate schools. Those are just two examples of the Court's power, and therefore, the president's power.

The reason why stores, restaurants and other pubic establishments are no longer permitted to ban our people from service is because of laws written by Congress, signed by the President, and later upheld by the USSC. That same pattern applied to state and local laws which required our people to pass certain tests and overcome other obstacles to simply be able to vote. Whether we are discussing the abolishment of slavery, the right of black men to vote (with obstacles later found to be unconstitutional), the right of women to vote, the civil rights movement, reproductive rights, homosexual rights, and criminal justice reform, you will see that society bends towards justice, and clearly bends toward the left; to the disdain of certain bigoted rightwing extremists who aim to oppress and control.

The perceived loss of power is a key reason for the rise of Donald J. Trump. He has tapped into this sense of entitlement, coupled with vitriolic anger, and he has galvanized a vocal group of people who claim to *want their country back*. Back to what? Trump espoused wanting to "make American great again" as the theme of his campaign. When do Trump and his ilk think America was great, exactly, and which demographics was it great for at that time?

Trump is a seventy-two-year-old, white, New York City based businessman, who has been a part of American culture for as long as I can remember. He inherited great wealth from his father and presided over a fortune built primarily through the business of real estate, among other ventures. Since I was a child, I recall hearing about his name and seeing his face. Up until this 2016 presidential election, Trump never formally entered politics. He has bragged about it being smart business sense for him over the years, to give donations to candidates in both the Democrat and Republican parties. He claims that he has voted for both Democrats and Republicans over the years. Regardless, he's always been a vile person. During the 2016 campaign for the presidency, Donald Trump continuously insulted women with disgusting words, in addition to mocking a handicapped person. The guy has viciously created a climate of hatred and fear against the Muslim community. On a weekly basis, his lies and gaffes cause his supporters and surrogates to explain away his conduct and privately try to get him to display some semblance of presidential credibility. The Obama presidency, along with his achievements and high approval rating, has caused certain demographics to lose their collective minds. They cannot fathom the prospect of losing power or accepting a more diverse society and power structure.

Trump's first key politically related opinion, which in retrospect was an early signal about how his mind works regarding race, was the infamous Central Park Five case from 1989. That was a famous case where five black and Hispanic youths were charged with brutally beating and raping a white woman in Central Park, in New York City. The case was well known both for the extreme violence, and the fact that race relations were at a combative point in the city. 1989 was the year of Spike Lee's *Do the Right Thing*.

On April 19, 1989, there were acts of violence throughout Central Park. The most vicious attack was on a white female jogger, who was raped and severely beaten to the point where she clung to her life while in a coma for twelve days. The attack made national news and it dominated the headlines in New York City. Five boys between the ages of fourteen and sixteen were detained and questioned for an extended period, while the police officers used intimidation and coercive tactics to gain "confessions." However, the "confessions" were retracted in the days after the interrogation and prior to their trials. During this tense time in New York, Donald J. Trump took out advertisements in four separate newspapers and used this case to call for the return of the death penalty in the State of New York.

After the boys were tried, convicted, and sentenced to prison, a serial rapist by the name of Matias Reyes confessed to the horrific crime. He was serving a life sentence in prison for other offenses. His admission was confirmed as true, when a test of the semen in the victim showed Reyes as the sole contributor. The five boys, now men, had their lives destroyed based on police malfeasance and malicious prosecution. They gave up a portion of their free lives-- between six and twelve years for all five boys--for a crime they did not commit. In September of 2014, the five boys collectively settled a $41 million suit against the City of New York. Donald Trump reacted to the settlement by doubling down on his belief in their guilt and called the settlement a "disgrace." Alas, this is Donald J. Trump for your consideration. It should be no surprise that Donald Trump settled a lawsuit with the federal government in the 1970s, for his refusal to allow blacks to live in some of his rental properties in New York City. Trump is a hero and inspiration for modern Nazis and white supremacists, who have become revitalized by his ascension.

Of course, Donald Trump unofficially started his foray into national politics by questioning the legitimacy of President Obama. Trump falsely claimed that President Obama was born in Kenya. This was an effort by Trump to otherize President Obama and make him seem less American. This racist birther movement, led by Trump, continued long after President Obama tried to pacify the racist portion of the populace by showing proof of his actual Hawaii issued birth certificate. Trump continued the smear for years later until in the middle of his campaign against Hillary Clinton, when the saner members of his team convinced him to give a brief statement to the press accepting that President Obama was indeed American born. The harassment of minorities and hate crimes rose sharply in the period following his election victory. Donald Trump has convinced and reminded certain white people that they are indeed the majority in this country, and that they should band together for a common interest; reinstating white men in power. That is why Donald Trump characterized some the Nazis and other white supremacists marching and chanting in Charlottesville, Virginia, as "very fine people."

Despite Trump's disgusting language and behavior toward women, 53% of white women voted Trump into office. http://www.cnn.com/election/results/exit-polls/national/president This same polling source also indicates that whites overwhelmingly voted for Trump, and that is no surprise as everything since the

Southern Strategy has taught us that white folks—particularly men-- are far more likely to vote Republican. However, though Hillary Clinton, former U.S. senator from New York, and later President Obama's Secretary of State, may have been an uninspiring candidate, she was certainly qualified for the job based on her wealth of experience. I have never been a huge Hillary Clinton fan, but I know she was the only candidate of the two who acknowledged a need for criminal justice reform. She admitted that there are racist elements in the criminal justice system, from the initial encounter with our people on the streets, and through the ultimate conviction and sentence.

Trump speaks of "law and order" and a need for more racist "stop and frisk" policies and procedures. I spent my time volunteering for Hillary Clinton's campaign in hopes for progressive policies that would lead to the decriminalization of marijuana, and a reduction in the masses of our people that remain incarcerated. I volunteered and voted for the Clinton campaign, because I did not want to imagine the unthinkable situation of President Obama shaking the hand of and handing over the beloved White House to this wicked man who long refused to acknowledge his presidency as deserved. Trump tried to completely delegitimize our first black president and he stoked racist hatred against him, and us. The Trump election would not have happened if a smart and motivated electorate had mobilized and exercised our right to vote in the manner that we did for President Obama.

We have the demographic support to absolutely vote him out of office in 2020. Stay-at-home apathy and wasteful third-party votes caused us to be stuck with Trump and the resurgence of vocal white supremacists. Moreover, Hillary won the popular vote in raw numbers by almost three million votes but lost because Trump held the edge with the Electoral College. Understand, that this means more people voted for Hillary Clinton than Trump. This is no time to bury our heads and feel all is lost, because that is not the case. Also, the Electoral College was decided by about 70,000 votes among states that Democrats typically win. The 2016 election was lost due to voter apathy and a failure to go to the polls to stop what seemed to be unthinkable. We as a people cannot allow this to ever happen again. Learn from this. Stay motivated and active. Freedom is not free.

It is particularly important to vote and get involved in politics that affect you at the local level. If your local county sheriff is not doing their job or is carrying it out in a corrupt and discriminatory manner, vote them out. The judges who are putting our people in prison for excessive sentences and administering decisions in a way that benefit law enforcement and big money law firms—entities that donate toward their reelection campaigns—should lose their seats on the bench. Other issues that affect our lives daily, such as the quality of your streets, zoning permits for businesses in your neighborhood, and countless other issues in the city are handled by elected officials whom you must hold accountable.

I went to my first city council meeting a while back in support of Tampa for Justice (TFJ). TFJ is an organization I became involved in rather organically. Ever since all the battles related to my sister's case ended in the summer of 2014, I've had a thirst to fight against injustice and corruption. I wanted to become more involved in my community on a political level. My day job fighting for the constitutional rights of my clients on death row, within the confines of the legal profession, did not and does not satiate my need to expose corruption and help vulnerable men, women, and particularly, children. One day I was looking at one of Tampa's community newspapers and read a short piece about a community forum addressing problems concerning the relationship between law enforcement and the urban community. I cut out the article and made a mental note to attend the gathering on the next Saturday morning.

The forum was in a packed local community center. The strained and dysfunctional relationship between local law enforcement and poor blacks has been an ongoing problem for decades. However, the catalyst for this meeting was the death of a local older black man while he was in police custody. The gentleman was driving his car erratically and once the officers caught up with him and detained him, he was in the process of dying of a diabetic seizure while in their custody. The forum lasted for several hours as panelists discussed ways to deal with the often-oppressive nature of community policing. Some of the speakers were filled with rage as they spoke about personal experiences with law enforcement. Others spoke of the issues with calls for patience and politicking. During my time there in the crowded room on a very rainy day, lots of pamphlets and flyers were handed out. One of those pieces of paper I carried with me to my car led me to another meeting a week or so later, held by a group called Tampa for Justice.

I learned that TFJ was put together to strive for justice and accountability on behalf of Tampa residents. The lit match that initially gave rise to the group was a local issue, perhaps scandal, which was gaining a lot of statewide attention. The Tampa police department was issuing more bicycle citations than any other law enforcement agency in the state. These infractions, often related to equipment, disproportionately affected the black community. The bias was so overwhelming on its face. After the Tampa Bay Times piece about the conduct became public, community pressure caused the mayor and police department to request an investigation from the U.S. Department of Justice.

So, I went to one meeting after another, until I decided to occasionally volunteer with this group as a part of my life. I took a vacation day from work and went to my first city council meeting while wearing my TFJ t-shirt. I was one of dozens to address the city council about the need to create a Civilian Review Board to handle complaints about police misconduct. I felt proud to be able to speak briefly from the heart. I've come to understand the importance of becoming politically active and involved with how our people are governed and controlled at the community level.

The Civilian Review Board matter is still unresolved, as the current model in place negotiated by our city council and mayor with various legal staff, is just political puppetry to protect city government from legitimate scrutiny. One of our next goals is for a properly resourced and legitimate review board, with subpoena power, to properly investigate citizen complaints and enforce accountability at the city level. It requires getting the requisite number of signatures from Tampa residents on a petition, to be placed on a ballot for vote during an upcoming election. This is democracy in action. I am not one of the leaders at TFJ and I do not attend every meeting. I make time when I can, and I donate my personal time and money when there is an issue, I am passionate about. I do appreciate taking part in a movement for social change. Besides TFJ, I also volunteer with my local ACLU chapter, as well as occasionally working with other social justice groups in the community.

One unacceptable, and frankly, immoral, voting related matter I was reminded about while attending meetings in the community involves the right of convicted felons to vote. Through my trips to TFJ meetings, I came across a flyer for a symposium about this topic I feel passionate about. The forum was being held at the University of Tampa; a beautiful campus close to downtown. While walking to the chapel where the event was held, I felt like I was in another land. Since I graduated from college twenty years ago, I've never really spent much time on any college campus, other than periodically attending football and basketball games at Ohio State. The college students walking amongst me looked so very young and child-like. I guess I never really spend a lot of time with younger people in their late teens and early twenties in large numbers. I felt bemused and old.

Once I arrived at the proper location, I read some literature about the ballot initiative permitting convicted felons the right to vote. I filled out and signed a petition, took a seat and soon had the pleasure of hearing from an engaging and inspiring man by the name of Desmond Meade. His story is phenomenal.

Desmond Meade grew up in South Florida and like a lot of black men of his generation; he struggled with aimlessness and drug addiction. After failing to find success in the Army or a meaningful career, his life began to fall apart as he engaged in a life of crime to support his addictions. Taking trips in and out of prison along with the death of his mother, caused Desmond to reach the lowest of low points in his life. In 2005, homeless, drug addicted, and losing faith in the meaning of his existence, Desmond Meade stood on train tracks waiting for a locomotive to end his misery. Fortunately for himself, and all of us, this extraordinary human being took a leap of faith off those tracks and immediately checked himself into a drug treatment program. This was his first step in taking ownership of himself and deciding that *he* deserved a better life.

Once Desmond successfully graduated from a drug treatment program, he moved into a local homeless shelter. Unwilling to let the humbling circumstances and close access to negative vices halt his momentum, Desmond enrolled in a local area college. Desmond Meade's criminal background served as a tool of improvement as opposed to a shackle of hindrance, as he majored in paralegal studies while graduating summa cum laude from a local Miami college. His interest in the legal field took him to Florida International Law School, from which he proudly graduated in 2014.

Desmond Meade is a success story. He represents the most admirable qualities of an American, or any human being for that matter; overcoming the odds and achieving personal redemption. Desmond and men and women like him, should be given every chance they can to succeed, thrive, and become leaders in our communities. Once a person pays their proverbial debt to society, by being incarcerated, monitored, fined, shamed, stripped of basic freedoms and dignity, they should not be forbidden from moving on past that dark period as they search for "morning in America." Unfortunately, Mr. Meade is not even permitted to utilize his law degree by sitting for the bar and practicing law in the State of Florida. A law was passed in Florida, which prevents convicted felons from practicing law.

Not only that, in Florida, along with nine other states, convicted felons were stripped of their right to vote, until the completion of a lengthy, and sometimes expensive process of trying to restore one's civil rights. In totality, all but two states in the country, Maine and Vermont, put some type of voting restriction on felons who are either incarcerated or under some type of probation or parole supervision. If you live in a state impacted by such laws, it is important for you to avoid becoming a convicted felon. If you are already a convicted felon make it a priority to get your civil rights restored, while simultaneously trying to get the existing oppressive laws changed. The aim of denying your right to vote is to strip you of your dignity. They are trying to make you feel like less of an American. Don't fall for that. Respect your personhood and fight back.

In Florida, concerned citizens indeed fought back. A proposed amendment to the Florida Constitution, Amendment 4, was placed on the ballot during the midterm elections of November2018. After a lengthy process that required a requisite number of signatures from Florida residents, along with a great deal of money and lobbying, Amendment 4 was voted into law by the citizens of Florida. This was a broad bipartisan effort, though those who opposed the law were on the conservative end of the political spectrum. In order to massage the language for mass consumption, the law only applies to felons who have not been convicted of murder or felony sex crimes. But once otherwise qualified convicted felons have completed the terms of their probation and parole, they are eligible to register to vote. This law affects at least 1.2 million people in Florida; disproportionately people of color. I am proud of my small part in volunteer efforts to help get the law passed. But the fight continues. Currently some conservatives in the Florida legislature are trying to figure out ways to create road blocks to limit the full impact of the new law. Another step will be educating affected convicted felons to exercise their right to vote in 2020 and beyond.

It is no accident or random occurrence that black Americans are always disproportionately affected by efforts to restrict felons from voting. You will hear about the term "purity of the ballot box" as a basis to deny people the most important and basic American freedom. What is impure are the motives of certain demographics who wish to guarantee that the white race remains in power, while many of our people are oppressed and scapegoated. The Fifteenth Amendment to the United States Constitution guaranteed our people the right to vote. Explicitly, the text of the Fifteenth Amendment reads as follows:

> **Section I.** The right of citizens of the United States to vote shall not be denied or abridged by the United States or by any State on account of race, color, or previous condition of servitude.

> **Section II.** The Congress shall have power to enforce this article by appropriate legislation.

However, as they are wont to do, certain racist demographics could not accept the prospect of true equality in voting. The initial rise of the Ku Klux Klan was fueled in part by resentment about the fact that black men would be exercising their rights as citizens. Literally, some white people would terrorize black communities through maiming and murder, to intimidate our people from voting. They tried to change the rules to suppress the vote. The grandfather clause prohibited descendants of slaves' ability to vote. Cost prohibitive poll taxes were pointedly used, along with "literacy tests" that white local officials would subjectively use against our people. This all lasted nearly a hundred years after the ratification of the Fifteenth Amendment.

Recall what was discussed in the previous chapter about Dr. King and Selma? The monumental march from Selma to Montgomery, Alabama was about suffrage. Dr. King realized the importance of rounding up our people to register to vote. Along with registration, the right to vote should be exercised without the obstacles and racist policies. Local bigoted goons, in law enforcement and civilians in the community, heckled and physically attacked Dr. King and fellow protesters to the point where the National Guard had to send troops to protect our people's right to walk in protest. The world watched, because Dr. King could understand the power of television cameras and publicity. Always remember the importance of shaming and exposure, along with the mobilizing to create an army of people to bring attention to the cause.

Zealous activism led to the Voting Rights Act of 1965. This Act has been extended multiple times by the federal government over the years. However, there have been continuous efforts by opponents of the Act to attempt to figure out ways to suppress the vote. This culminated with the dangerous <u>Shelby v. Holder</u> decision of 2013. The crux of the case is that the court's 5-4 decision invalidated section 4(b) of the Voting Rights Act of 1965, which required a coverage formula for certain jurisdictions based on their legacy of voting abridgement or depravation. Section (5) supported section 4 (b) by requiring preclearance by the federal government—the U.S Attorney General or a three-judge panel of the D.C.'s United States district court—before any state or local government could make changes to their voting laws or practices. These federal actors were supposed to make sure that such local changes did not deny or abridge our people's voting rights, or those otherwise defined by a race, color, or language minority group. Along partisan lines, the conservatives on the United States Supreme Court determined that section 4(b) was outdated and no longer necessary under its original formulation.

Conservatives in Congress who spent eight years trying to obstruct most all policies supported by President Obama, have failed to modernize the Voting Rights Act to protect modern day minorities. Instead, what you are seeing are efforts to restrict the

For Black Men/Ali Shakoor

votes of those who are statistically more likely to vote for a Democrat. Across the country, Republican led local governments have passed what have become known as "voter ID" laws. Objectively, the concept seems simple enough. There is an unsubstantiated belief held by some that voter fraud is rampant and some type of photo identification is needed to insure the concept of "one person, one vote." Oh really? Will these zealots mandate there is a process in place to make sure the identification cards are free, and there is some type of mobile service to provide cards to impoverished communities? Otherwise, such laws do exactly what opponents fear; they limit the ability of poor people, often black, who are less likely to have photo identification. Requiring a person to pay for identification is tantamount to the sordid poll taxes of the past. Voting is a fundamental right. It is not a privilege.

Other efforts to limit the votes of our people are more blatant. Many black churches across the country make a special effort to bus people to voting booths from church on election days. This is a special event, particularly considering our history and the role the black church served in the civil rights movement. Yet, in the past several years, states, including swing states like Ohio and Florida, have tried to eliminate voting on the Sunday before Election Day. Similar efforts were made in Wisconsin, Nevada, and North Carolina.

Some Republicans blatantly admit concerns about our people voting. I suppose they forgot how to use code. In September 2011, a Georgia state senator by the name of Fran Miller wrote an angry opinion piece about the opportunities afforded our people to vote on Sunday, in a mall in a predominantly black neighborhood. In August2012, Ohio Republican chair, Doug Pries, stated "I guess I really actually feel we shouldn't contort the voting process to accommodate the urban — read African-American — voter-turnout machine." Here is another one, in an effort to apparently turn back the clock on civil rights in this country, a Florida Republican running for a seat in the House of Representatives in 2012by the name of Ted Yoho, stated a desire for only property owners to be allowed to vote. Yoho later tried to backtrack and say he was only making a "historical reference." Find details about these statements and more, here. https://billmoyers.com/2014/10/24/voter-discrimination/

Since the shortsighted <u>Holder</u> decision, federal appellate courts have overturned legislation in states which have attempted to limit the ability of black people to vote. These federal judges, some even appointed by Republican presidents, have reversed these crude and bigoted laws which have served no purpose, other than to make it harder for black people to vote. In fact, these racist state legislators requested data on when and how particular demographics vote, and then tailored their legislation for the sole purpose of making voting difficult for our people by reducing early voting, mandating a particular type of photo ID requirement, and eliminating same day registration, among other restrictions.

https://www.npr.org/sections/thetwo-way/2016/07/29/487935700/u-s-appeals-court-strikes-down-north-carolinas-voter-id-law

This is shameful and enraging. Remember, our people, along with good people of other races, have literally risked and lost lives in the fight for suffrage. These particular conservatives could try to expand their base by reexamining their message. They could try to become more open-minded and inclusive. Instead, their greed and bigotry are causing them to attempt to rollback everything that the good people on both political sides have fought for and accomplished. No wonder many rightwing conservatives are so hostile to the federal government. The feds serve as a check on their power to inflict bigoted policies. When you hear coded language referring to "states' rights," please understand that it's the same type of garbage that was peddled during the Jim Crow era, which has now been watered down for public consumption in mixed company.

The late Lee Atwater, a rightwing Republican mastermind, took part in an interview in 1981which gave away secrets to how some rightwing conservatives have used race to divide the country and deny rights for our people

For Black Men/Ali Shakoor

<u>*https://www.thenation.com/article/exclusive-lee-atwaters-infamous-1981-interview-southern-strategy/*</u>:

You start out in 1954 by saying, "Nigger, nigger, nigger." By 1968 you can't say "nigger"—that hurts you, backfires. So, you say stuff like, uh, forced busing, states' rights, and all that stuff, and you're getting so abstract. Now, you're talking about cutting taxes, and all these things you're talking about are totally economic things and a byproduct of them is, blacks get hurt worse than whites.... "We want to cut this," is much more abstract than even the busing thing, uh, and a hell of a lot more abstract than "Nigger, nigger."

Always keep this quote in mind, and do not get fooled by the evil game those folks are trying to play on us. Stay vigilant. Demand the right to vote, without encumbrances. It is our most important right.

My obvious point here is the fact that the fundamental rights that our elders and ancestors, literally, put their lives on the line for, are under attack. It is pathetic and evil. Make sure to take advantage of the opportunity to vote. Think about the problems that directly impact you, your family and your community. Imagine the type of world you want to live in. Then research the candidates that are most willing and able to create positive results.

I should also make the point that I am not trying to steer you toward a specific political party or agenda. Unfortunately, this country is dominated by a two-party system. That limits the options and the leverage we have as a people. Frankly, both parties have blood on their hands, literally, for what they've done to our race. I have discussed recent and current Republicans who have been blatantly disrespectful and oppressive towards us. But we are a diverse people with distinct interests and belief systems. Personally, I have some viewpoints that may be on the conservative end of the spectrum, but on some other topics, particularly social issues, I tend to be more progressive. I want you to get involved and stay engaged, and this is particularly because America is a majority white collection of folks, many who want to maintain their grip on the political power structure.

Donald Trump is probably our most racially divisive president since Woodrow Wilson. There is a reason why white supremacists have been celebrating all over the country. About a week after the election, alt-right white nationalists held a celebratory rally in our nation's Capital, in a building named after Ronald Reagan, where they yelled "Heil Trump!" It is important for our people to develop ourselves by controlling what we can: focus on self-improvement, be determined to stay out of the system, and intelligently fight back against oppression every step of the way.

The Clintons are not nearly as shamelessly race-baiting as Trump. However, Hillary Clinton supported her husband's efforts in the 1990s to put poorer, urban, black people in jail, which led to a massive spike in our nation's prison population. During Bill Clinton's presidency, in support of his efforts to increase the prison population with laws such as the infamous "three strikes" atrocities, Hillary Clinton referred to young urban youths who committed crimes as "super predators," who needed to be brought "to heel." When Barack Obama was running against Hillary Clinton in 2008, the Clintons were in shock. Here was a self-identified black man named Barack Hussein Obama, who was spoiling what the Clintons thought would be her coronation to the Democratic nomination. President Obama actually worked the streets of Chicago as a community organizer during his first forays into the political realm. President Obama could see directly how systematic racism, weaponized with the War on Drugs and housing discrimination, had created a sense of hopelessness. He took the optics with him to law school and fed his already enriched history of our black experience. He left law school and shortly thereafter entered politics looking to improve his local community as a state senator, then as a U.S. senator, and then as the 44th president of these United States.

You know another interesting issue regarding Trump and the Clintons? Trump cleaned up a lot of Bill Clinton's racist mess of a crime bill by signing The First Step Act into law. The full name of the law is the Formerly Incarcerated Reenter Society Safely Transitioning Every Person Act. It was passed with broad bipartisan support, but for twelve Republicans who voted against it. This law does not go far enough, and there is some frustration about how long it is taking to implement certain aspects, but it's still the most sweeping federal criminal justice reform signed into law in a long damn time. Already, some prisoners have been released to their families after serving unjust sentences. Think about how an investment into political advocacy and hope has cashed in for these folks. Among the many reforms, the law places more of an emphasis on rehabilitation and increases the opportunity toward more time credits for eligible inmates. The law isn't enough, but it is surely better than nothing. It also shows how "evolving standards of decency" can compel some lawmakers to do the right thing. I don't care if Trump signed the law to spite the Clintons, to stick it to Obama who never got a chance to sign such legislation because the Republicans in Congress didn't want him to have the achievement, or because his family and advisors changed his heart for the better, if at least this one time. What matters are the results that help our people.

I am not trying to tell you who to vote for or what party to support. I have views that fall on both sides of the political aisle. I have voted for Republicans in more localized elections, but conservatives need to stop dog-whistling and otherwise appealing to racists nationwide. There is a reason why self-avowed white supremacists not only more often vote Republican, but also run as Republican candidates when seeking office themselves; they like what they hear and see on the right. Our political system does not provide more options, like those found in many foreign countries. America's two-party system limits the incentive of those in power to be willing to accommodate and share, as they often rather fill a desire to oppress and control. We work with what we have. It is still crucially important to vote. The qualities and policies of politicians' matter. Follow your conscious and belief system. Travel whatever political path best impacts your life in an enriching and positive way. Do not support bullies and bigots. More specifically, actively vote against politicians who support or traffic in oppression. Take advantage of your voice and rights. Do not allow evil folks to suppress your vote.

Freedom is not free. Do not expect oppressive white supremacy to fall without a fight from those who plan to protect their power and privilege. The election of 2016 was an extremely crucial wake-up call. Get politically involved, because our progress and survival depend on it. People just need to remember to vote, and vote in an educated manner.

Chapter Five

<u>Beware of Demons</u>

"Brown had the most intense aggressive face. The only way I can describe it, it looks like a demon, that's how angry he looked." That was an excerpt from former Ferguson, Missouri police officer, Darren Wilson's grand jury testimony, explaining why he fatally shot unarmed Michael Brown six times on August 9, 2014, during a physical struggle, before leaving the teenager's corpse in the blood-stained streets. Michael's body lay in the street for four hours. Referring to Michael as a "demon" is an interesting choice of words by Darren Wilson. It is also the type of language and imagery used by whites in America for centuries to justify extreme violence and the outright murder of black men and boys.

Once you dehumanize a person, it makes the murder of them seem justified or unimportant. What a demonic way of thinking and only "demons" think this way. That is how my late grandfather, Andrew Jordan characterized the *real* demons in law enforcement, and so did his father, Clevester Jordan, and so did my maternal grandfather, Hamp Love. They each had witnessed the savage beatings of unarmed blacks who were complying, and it was widely known in the South which police officers were members of the Ku Klux Klan who murdered blacks. During the 1960s, my grandfather was the only schoolteacher openly active in the Greenwood, Mississippi civil rights movement; and he was field secretary, under Medgar Evers, for the Greenwood Chapter of the *National Association for the Advancement of Colored People* (NAACP).Like many black boys, I grew up with this knowledge and lessons about how to survive racism within law enforcement. I am not afraid to speak up about cowardly, racist, demon cops who hate black people. We must speak up. What is happening is morally reprehensible. It is the truth that for centuries black men, women and children have been terrorized by fear of demons, within law enforcement that are supposed to be protectors of all Americans. In my family, every generation of black men have witnessed live in person, and in my generation on the news, a televised beating or the murder of unarmed blacks by police officers.

There are still some demons patrolling our streets. Please be very careful. They are getting away with murdering black people and this is infuriating. Good cops and honorable cops have had their hands sullied as well, because law enforcement agencies tend to stick together (Code Blue) or become vulnerable to retaliation. The FBI is aware about the problem of white supremacists infiltrating local law enforcement agencies all over the country.

https://www.pbs.org/newshour/nation/fbi-white-supremacists-in-law-enforcement

I want you to be aware of the real "demons" in this country, who will kill you and then later fabricate a narrative to justify their murder. Be careful out there, because American law enforcement is out of control. There is a whole culture of demon cops, and other officers know about them, and not enough is being done to remove them from the ranks. I am not going to sit here and lie to you and tell you that 99.9% or even *most* law enforcement officers are unbiased, have integrity and are fair. I honestly do not know what the number or amount may be. And despite what you hear from politicians and pundits, they do not know either. These protectors of the shield in some instances are simply idealistic or naïve. In other cases, some vocal protectors of the shield have an agenda to always defend police and deflect from their egregious biased conduct because they are racists, and others are bootlicking Uncle Toms.

I do know that it is fair and honest to state that being a law enforcement officer is a difficult job, and many do their jobs honorably, honestly, and free from bias. On the other hand, some of these gutless demons will think nothing of taking your life, due to cowardice, or a simple indefensible desire to kill black people and get away with it.

During January 2018, in Prospect, Kentucky a high-ranking demon cop who apparently has a deep hatred for blacks, and a lack of respect for the rule of law, he lost his job in law enforcement, and tarnished his over twenty-year career. Assistant Police Chief Todd Shaw was caught instructing a Louisville recruit on how to handle black people. His message was vulgar, hate filled and indefensible. He wrote, "If they are black shoot them." When asked by the recruit if a juvenile was found smoking marijuana, he wrote, "Fuck doing the right thing. If mom is hot then fuck her. If the dad is hot, handcuff him and make him suck my dick. Unless daddy is black shoot him." Assistant Police Chief Todd Shaw wrote all this, and more on his personal Facebook post. It was supposed to have been private, but someone retrieved his Facebook account, found this filth, and the county prosecutor got involved. After the mayor investigated, Shaw was suspended and then fired. The following is an excerpt and quote highlighting an outstanding message from Jefferson County, U.S. Attorney, Mike O'Connell: https://www.courier-Journal.com/story/news/2018/01/19/prospect-police-officer-racist-messages-kill-blacks/1048979001/*"O'Connell also said it was "quite disturbing that Shaw, a senior law enforcement officer with more than 20 years' experience, was expressing his offensive racist views with a young recruit training to be a Louisville Metro Police officer."*

The county attorney's office said it would move to dismiss two dozen District Court cases in which Shaw was the sole witness, regardless of whether the defendants were black.

O'Connell told reporters Friday that Shaw was terminated and that the recruit — who was not identified — wasn't hired by Louisville Metro.

Rejecting Shaw's bid to keep the messages private, Jefferson Circuit Judge Judith McDonald Burkman ruled Thursday that they revealed "prejudices that bring into question Shaw's integrity as a law enforcement officer" and that public concern was "magnified by his rank."

O'Connell told reporters that his office supports police officers "but this kind of person walking the streets of this community with a gun or badge should never be tolerated. And they should be weeded out, for all our good."

What Shaw did was racist and appalling. All over our country, taxpayers are footing the bill when million-dollar civil judgments are won in court, and then paid out to grieving black families. When unarmed blacks are killed by cops, you're going to need a clear video of the murder, and even then, that may not be enough for a conviction. As a quick aside, folks who are anxious to deflect to "black on black crime" can kiss my whole black ass. When blacks kill other blacks, they are prosecuted and sent to prison without the need for video evidence. This is justice; and tens of thousands of white, black and brown Americans are not protesting in streets across the country when there is justice.

Prior to killing Michael Brown, Officer Darren Wilson arrested a man in 2013, who was legally filming and recording him. He tried to get the man charged with "failure to comply." Prior to arresting the civilian, Wilson lied to the man and told him that he was not within his rights in filming him, a police officer. The charges were eventually dropped. That is Darren Wilson, for you. *https://www.theguardian.com/us-news/2014/nov/16/ferguson-video-shows-darren-wilson-arresting-man-for-recording-him*

From what we know about the day in question that led to Michael Brown's murder, Brown had allegedly stolen something at a local convenience store. By the time Wilson encountered Brown, Wilson had knowledge that Brown may be a suspect in the crime at the convenience store. A verbal altercation ensued regarding Brown walking in the middle of the street, followed by a physical altercation. The local grand jury and the U.S. Department of Justice eventually cleared Wilson of any wrongdoing, under the assumption that Michael Brown decided to apparently commit suicide by running into a storm of bullets. Of course, Wilson did not shoot to maim Michael Brown, and nor did he use a taser on him in hopes to subdue him for an arrest. He shot Brown six times. A simple Google search will show you multiple videotaped examples of white people waving guns at officers, who are eventually taken into custody alive. To some police officers, a white person threatening officers with an actual gun must have more humanity and value as a life worth saving, than an angry and weaponless black teenager.

When I was a public defender, I once represented a young white man from Michigan. His grandmother called me daily. She was worried sick about him. He was 18 or 19 years old, temporarily living in Tampa with friends, and thinking of starting a new life down South. One night, his mix of homesickness and a ridiculous level of alcohol started him on a drunken wander in the middle of a late-night street. He was in full blackout mode and does not remember a thing, but according to the police reports the officers saw how intoxicated he was and tried to execute something called a Marchman Act. In Florida, a Marchman Act basically involves a law enforcement officer taking a person into temporary custody, because the civilian's obvious display of public intoxication may cause them to be a danger to themselves or others.

When the officers encountered my client, he was non-compliant. More so than that, he started fighting the officers like a madman, like a "demon." My client had charged and fought two officers at the same time. He punched and kicked and spat on them. If I recall correctly, I believe he was also tased several times. After a great deal of struggle, a spit guard was placed on him, and he was eventually arrested, and charged with multiple counts of battery on a law enforcement officer. The officers did not shoot my client. They did not take out their batons and beat him until he was nearly deformed or left with broken bones. The kid lived. And, I was also able to creatively get him a plea offer which kept him from becoming a convicted felon. My client's probation was transferred back to his home state of Michigan where his grandmother was waiting to set him straight.

If Michael Brown did indeed decide to charge at an armed police officer, one should wonder what could trigger such rage. The community where Michael Brown's incident occurred, Ferguson, Missouri, is a majority black community which had long been locally renowned for police officers treating our people with biased and hostile methods. Even though Darren Wilson was legally cleared of charges for the murder of Michael Brown, the U.S Department of Justice decided that there was enough evidence and citizen accounts to conduct a federal investigation of the Ferguson police department. In the spring of 2015, the Justice Department found that the local police force regularly policed in a discriminatory manner. *http://www.nytimes.com/2015/03/04/us/justice-department-finds-pattern-of-police-bias-and-excessive-force-in-ferguson.html?smid=pl-share&_r=0*. The police department was targeting our people for trivial offenses like jaywalking, and grossly disproportionately stopping our people for traffic offenses, resulting in tickets and arrests. Moreover, the few times when whites were charged with similar crimes, they were about three times more likely to have their cases dismissed. The Justice Department was compelled to sue Ferguson, Missouri. On March 17, 2016, the city of Ferguson and the Justice Department entered a settlement agreement. *https://www.justice.gov/opa/pr/justice-department-and-city-ferguson-missouri-resolve-lawsuit-agreement-reform-ferguson*.

Ferguson was tasked with implementing reforms via a fourteen-point plan of action. Unfortunately, the consent decree only required two years of compliance before the agreement could be terminated, but we can only hope that Ferguson, Missouri is scared straight so to speak, or shamed into exercising their authority in a non-divisive and race-neutral fashion going forward. It is tragic that Michael Brown was alive in Ferguson under such oppressive conditions. Racism is enraging. It can devastate, causing emotional pain and anger, as you try to fight back; weaponless, beyond pride and a desire for freedom. This is probably what happened with Sandra Bland and Eric Garner, and sadly, far too many more to name.

Police corruption and blatant systematic racism was also uncovered by the DOJ in Baltimore, Maryland. The protests and anger in Baltimore were not only the result of the brutal death of

Freddie Gray, while in police custody, which resulted in the city of Baltimore paying a $6.4 million settlement to Gray's family. The American citizens in Baltimore were also disgusted with the Baltimore police department being permitted to continuously violate the constitutional rights, and hurl racial slurs at our people with impunity. Here, you can read how some of the demon thugs in the city of Baltimore treat its black citizens, our people, as if we are not entitled to the protections of the United States Constitution and must instead live as less than second class citizens:*https://assets.documentcloud.org/documents/3009376/BPD-Findings-Report-FINAL.pdf*

You can also read there how the so-called "good cops" stood silent while the brutality and corruption happen. On the rare occasions when a "good cop" does speak up to file complaints and seek accountability, they are threatened, and the complaints are whitewashed. It is a rigged system, but it is important to keep fighting. The death of Freddie Gray led to the protests and advocacy, which in turn led to the federal investigation. I would hope to see more reforms to be put in place, like what occurred in Ferguson, Baltimore, and few other American cities, except the Trump administration has no desire to hold corrupt and racist municipalities accountable.

Eric Garner was simply selling loose cigarettes before he was literally choked to death by members of the New York City police department. Sandra Bland was smoking one, before she was arrested and later died under mysterious circumstances while in police custody. Their anger played into the demonic hands of certain law enforcement officers.

Look, I am going to tell you something you have probably heard before, but I hope you will consider the gravity of my words with the utmost seriousness:

Whenever you encounter law enforcement, please keep your anger subdued and make the episode as brief as possible.

By stating this, I am not asking you to kiss ass, lick boots, or deny yourself your innate sense of dignity. I am not even telling you to use the words ma'am or sir. I am just stating that you may be dealing with a possible demon that is looking for a chance to shoot you. You could be encountering a coward, who fears our blackness. Follow the instructions of law enforcement and keep your hands visible at all times. Philando Castile, that name may be entering your mind. What about him, you may ask, as he followed the instructions of the cowardly and confusingly hyper police officer and was still murdered in cold blood in front of his fiancé and a small child. That is a murder which proves my point. Some demons out in the streets are just looking for a reason to shoot you. The Castile tragedy is an extremely rare occurrence. Most police murders of our people involve some type of struggle or "resisting." The cowardly demon who shot Mr. Castile was acquitted because he is a cop, and that is usually what happens when cops shoot our people. He was however, fired and shamed as his actions were even condemned by some conservative minded folks, who usually tend to worship and believe all cops. The Castile family and his fiancé eventually received money in a civil settlement. They would rather have him alive.

Resisting a lawful, unlawful or unjustified arrest, is a natural human instinct. You can see such an occurrence happen on nearly every episode of *Cops*. Resisting arrest does not mean you deserve to be murdered. But it does give law enforcement the option of a distraction and a sense of cover, which also applies to your local prosecutors who rarely ever prosecute police officers for crimes against our people.

Prosecutors work arm in arm with law enforcement. They are reliant upon each other for the successful prosecution of crimes. Prosecutors also have a self-serving interest in career advancement. They depend on police unions for support and votes.

Tamir Rice was murdered by a demon of a police officer who essentially committed a common drive-by shooting on the young boy. One chilly day in Cleveland, Ohio during a time of the year that seemed to fall between that period of autumn colors and the vast whiteness of winter, a rookie police officer with a documented history of emotional problems and his "mentor" responded at a park to investigate a call about a man walking around pointing a gun at people and objects. When they arrived at the scene there was no calling for backup and beginning a dialogue with Tamir Rice, you know, like you see officers engage white suspects with actual real guns. The police car screeched to a halt, and the cop with a history of being emotionally unstable murdered twelve-year-old Tamir Rice as he played in the park with his toy gun. Tamir was never given a chance to respond or react. The entire episode lasted less than two seconds. Tamir's sister was also in the park with him. When she saw that her brother had been shot, the crazed demons handcuffed the young teen as if she were a common criminal, as opposed to a grieving and traumatized child.

If you are familiar with the American grand jury system, you understand that it is very easy for a prosecutor to achieve an indictment. A common joke goes along the lines of the fact than any decent prosecutor could indict a ham sandwich. The grand jury process in largely one-sided, usually done in secret, and has an extremely low threshold of which a prosecutor needs to overcome to achieve an indictment. What is noticeable about the Tamir Rice case, however, is the fact that the county prosecutor actively tried to avoid seeking an indictment during the grand jury process. He effectively acted as a defense attorney for the officers involved. It would be disingenuous to say the prosecutor's actions were unprecedented, because as we discussed, state attorneys actively try to protect police officers from prosecution all over the country. But the extent to which the prosecutor in the Tamir Rice case bent over backwards to protect this police officer during the grand jury process was just a shameful situation. It adds credence to the belief that police officers are often truly above the law. Such behavior only fosters resentment in the urban community. Police officers and those who support them, often feign concern about fostering positive relationships between cops and blacks in urban communities but refuse to hold police officers accountable for misconduct against our people. Laws need to be passed which would take prosecutorial control out of hands of local prosecutors, when there are allegations of violence perpetrated by law enforcement. Somebody from the federal government, or a statewide prosecutor lacking any local political ties should handle such cases.

These demons rarely face any accountability, and therefore it is crucial for you to protect yourself from them. Comply. Keep your hands up always. Please check your local laws regarding the recording and filming of law enforcement, as that is often the only means of achieving some level of accountability.

In 2015, a corrupt demon shot a black man by the name of Walter Scott in the back, while Scott was fleeing from the scene of an arrest in South Carolina. The demon then tried to change the crime scene to make it look like Mr. Scott had possession of a weapon. If there was not video of this incident, the demon cop never would have been convicted, and the local authorities probably would have believed the lie-filled account in the police report.

Similarly, video that high ranking government officials in the City of Chicago tried to suppress showed the cold-blooded murder of a troubled and drugged up young man named Laquan McDonald. The actual video, along with the testimony of some honest officers, led to the conviction of the demon who shot Mr. McDonald. Without video, the murderous cop would still be on the streets today. It is important to avoid being out in the world with gun-toting demons, while you are too inebriated to understand what is going on and unable to obey orders. Even if you're sober you must control your rage and stay calm.

Understand, when I mention the need to comply and avoid resisting arrest, this does not mean you need to swallow your anger and choke on it. It is about staying alive. It is about staying out of the judicial system. Recently, someone uploaded a video online of a young brother being tased by an officer who had mistaken him for someone else with an active warrant. The scared brother refused to get out of the car when asked, so the officer tased the shit out of him before finally becoming aware that he had the wrong man. But the brother still faced an obstruction charge and a possible violation of his first offender probation for a prior minor drug possession charge. He could get a criminal record, which limits the type of work he can do and where he can live. Swallow your fear and anger and comply. This does not mean you should take it! Just channel your energy into getting back another way. Write letters to supervisors and internal affairs, because despite how corrupt and protective police departments may often be, it never hurts to file a complaint, which becomes a part of the officer's file. Mobilize a protest. Protests do not have to be on your behalf, just because you are dead, or in jail because of the actions of law enforcement. You can organize a protest yourself, based on how you have been treated.

I allowed my anger about the mistreatment of my niece and family to negatively affect my career and almost drive me into a rage. Instead, I should have spent that energy organizing a community to fight the injustice and by creating a website to expose it. My grandmother has a website on my family's behalf now; exposing everything those folks in Ohio did to us. Knowing that those folks' family, friends, colleagues, and other concerned citizens can read about their actions, makes me feel a lot better than sitting around mad; going off the handle to my own detriment. Fight back intelligently. A cool head always prevails. Keep it short, stay alive, and stay out of the system. Get back at them in other ways, or if it is not worth your time and energy, enjoy your life free of confinement or supervision, and consider this to be a small victory itself.

Black people have a reason to be pissed off about how we are treated by the judicial system. I have had black clients who were the victims of reckless and prejudicial treatment. For brevity, I can recall two experiences vividly. They both involved black men picked up off the streets, arrested, and given bonds they could not afford. They were victims of those ridiculous controlled buy/bust incidents, where there is a videotaped undercover buy and the arrest is made days later. In both incidents—one guy in his 20s and the other in his early 50s—thcy were treated like garbage at the time of the arrest and a later viewing of the videotapes showed plain as day that is was mistaken identity. It was not even close. In the situation with the younger guy, I finally got the assistant state attorney, a young white woman of Cuban descent, to watch the tape with her boss after a couple pretrial dates, and she dropped the charges. Imagine sitting locked up in jail for something you did not do. It's frightening and infuriating.

The other guy, an older gentleman, he had a family to provide for at home. I could not get the particular assistant state attorney, a black woman, to drop the charges based on a viewing of the tape. On the morning of trial, I told the judge how this was a case of obvious mistaken identity. The judge, a very experienced Jewish woman, asked to watch the video for herself. After watching the incident on video, which clearly showed a black man different in age and complexion than my client, the judge told us that she would be happy to quickly dispose of this case with a non-jury trial. The assistant state attorney, getting the hint, and wanting to protect her stats, quickly offered to get approval from her supervisor to dismiss the case. Great, the case was dismissed. This is all fine and dandy, except my client was locked away from his family for a couple months, and he lost his job. The reckless disregard for black lives by some in law enforcement and by many prosecutors is absolutely infuriating. It can often feel demoralizing, but it is important to fight back in intelligent fashion.

I took part in a rally on behalf of the Joseph family during the 2015 Florida State Fair, because law enforcement was responsible for the death of their son, who died due to the egregious conduct of the Hillsborough County Sheriff's Office. The death of their son has created some reforms and the family deserves to receive a substantial civil settlement, but that will not bring young "Pee-Wee" back from the dead. I'll explain what happen.

The Florida State Fair has a racist history. During the period of Jim Crow, our people were not permitted to attend the fair, but the white folks figured out a way to get black money by patronizing us with something known as Negro Day. Negro Day evolved into something called Student Day, which was a day where students are to take the day off school and spend money at the fair. Parents are working during the period when children are at school, so the situation resulted in hundreds of children at the fair without any adult supervision.

During the chaos of kids, some members of local gangs, running around the fair unsupervised, young Andrew Joseph III was among numerous students rounded up and processed for possible gang affiliations and/or warrants. Andrew was not a gang member. He was an honor student, who was not taking part in any illegal activity. Andrew was a victim of racial profiling and a disregard for human dignity. He was asked to bare his chest to prove that he did not have any tattoos showing gang affiliations. Andrew remained in the custody of the Hillsborough County Sheriff's department until they decided to release him. What happen next was just a shameless example of negligence and a disregard for black children. Instead of calling young Andrew's parents, Andrew Joseph, Jr. and mother,

Deanna, the deputies simply dropped the fourteen-year-old child off on the side of the freeway, more than a mile from the fair. They had no regard for his safety and well-being. Young Andrew was killed when struck by a vehicle as he attempted to cross the freeway back to the familiar territory of the fair, where a neighbor was due to pick him up.

I attended the protest at the fairgrounds, on one of the anniversaries of Pee-Wee's tragic death. There were dozens of people present there on that chilly afternoon in support of the Joseph family. Different races and ages were chanting about overcoming oppression and exposing injustice. There was a police presence in the form of the local deputies from the same agency that was responsible for young Andrew's death, and different uniforms I did not recognize which I was later told were from the "feds." There was no agitation from law enforcement that afternoon. However, a few of the protesters grew angry with the some of the officers due to their very existence. A black officer was particularly subjected to verbal abuse. He was called a sellout and an Uncle Tom. The deputy stayed calm and kept it all professional. What I found frustrating was the fact that such hostility is simply not productive. We as black people always lament over the fact that our race is under represented in local law enforcement. Well, right there was a brother who was representing the community in a professional manner, and yet, was berated for it.

Maybe he joined the force to make a positive difference. The treatment of this officer by only a few, out of dozens of protestors, was my cue to leave as the protest event was concluding anyway.

Anger, insults and aggression are losing methods for our people when encountering law enforcement. I understand the anger and resentment. I do. But it must be channeled into something more productive. Taunting a police officer not only makes you a target for future retribution, it turns off less radical supporters who are absolutely, positively, and goddamn essential in helping the cause. Needless to say, the murder of a police officer is wicked and cowardly; as is the advocating of such. If our elders from the civil rights era from decades ago chose the path of instigation, violence, and inciting violence, we would not have the gains achieved for our people over the past several decades. Jim Crow would still be in place in some fashion, and no matter how bad things are, objectively, it is not as bad for us in America, as when King and others started the movement over sixty years ago. We must combat oppression with brains and exposure. Use the law to your advantage and never give up. We represent about 13% of the U.S. population, so it is not like South Africa where we can rise up and just start taking over the country by any means necessary. We need help and support from those who are believers in equality and righteous, who happen to represent the majority white race. We always have and always will need that support

Also, it is important to note that not all of law enforcement are the enemy. They are not all wicked and corrupt; too many, but not all. I know some demographics will take issue with my use of the words "demon" or "thug." It does not apply in blanket fashion to all cops, but rather only the ones who think nothing of taking a black life for no good reason at all. It applies to cops who our racist, dishonest, corrupt, and ones who refuse to follow the law. As certain demographics call our people hoodlums or thugs, or worse, when we are violent, well then, a cowardly murderous cop can wear a demonic thug label. Because only the lowest form of humanity would have behaved like the demon who shot Tamir Rice, or the one who shot Walter Scott in the back, or the others across the nation who have lost their jobs for sadistic brutality, or racist language and/or have membership with the KKK. Never forget, blatantly racist cops still freely work all over the United States.

When I was a young public defender, the first case I handled on my own involved a pre-teen juvenile and a police officer. I believe the charge was something insignificant, relatively, about my client allegedly refusing to stop on his motorized bike when the officer allegedly tried to execute a stop. I state the word "insignificant" in the context of the overall criminal punishment exposure, but this issue certainly was not "insignificant" for my young client and his family, dealing with the anxiety of criminal prosecution for the first time. The facts in the police report and my client's testimony clearly indicated that my client was targeted and had done nothing wrong. This trial, referred to as an adjudicatory hearing for juvenile law purposes, was before a judge. Though an inexperienced attorney, I successfully cross-examined the cop to the point that he was clearing lying. At one point at the end of my closing summation, the judge did something that my black supervisor had never seen before. The judge asked to read the police report. Based on the rules of evidence this was not proper, but I complied with the judge's request. After perusing the brief report, the judge immediately found my client not guilty. That judge previously had a reputation for being pro-state, like most judges. Yet he was a conservative, white, Hispanic judge ruling in favor of a young black boy, and taking his word over a southern good ole' boy cop. I will always remember that case, but mostly for the conversation with my supervisor that followed it.

Not with a scolding tone, but rather, with parental concern, this supervisor complimented me for winning the case while offering advice concerning my tactics. The black supervisor remarked that I was from up north, Ohio, and that in the future it may be wise for a black attorney like me, to not make a white cop look like a liar on the stand. The supervisor stated that racism is still prevalent in Tampa, and that some white judges and juries may resent a black attorney making a white cop look like the liar he or she is. Rather, and this was just career related advice, the supervisor cautioned me to make *lying* cops appear as they simply made a *mistake* in their reporting. I nodded although perplexed, and I thought about it for the rest of the day, but by the time I got home I decided, "Fuck that shit!" My instincts proved correct during that case, and my character simply would not allow me to worry about the perceptions of lying and/or racist cops. I will never stop helping our young people get over the hurdles of racist and overzealous law enforcement. Lying and corrupt cops need to be exposed and removed from employment. I am not afraid of white people. Most of them do the right thing. I am from "up North!" Whatever. I was raised to have racial pride, and not to lick boots, and abet white supremacy which is the root of demon cops. They believe that a black person's life is worth nothing. Well, I was taught that we have value and that injustice is wrong and immoral. This is why I became a defense attorney.

There are men and women in law enforcement who work hard to do an undeniably rough job with honor and bravery. They should be commended and treated with respect. When encountering a police officer, your being calm and respectful is not just necessary for your survival, it is a display of humanity to treat any fellow human being with calm and recognition of the "Golden Rule."

Some officers are even willing to use discretion and give compassionate breaks to citizens. Fortunately, I have only had a few encounters with law enforcement in my life. Not only was I treated properly and professionally, I also have received huge, huge breaks from police officers. In late summer of 2002, I was arrested for the first and only time in my life. I was wrong and I completely deserved it. Before I became enlightened, I used to be a drunk driver. And, like too many drunk drivers who think they know it all, that was how my friends and I rolled. We were ignorant and reckless, but at the time if I was awake and able to walk, I considered myself able to drive. But I left my friend's bachelor party under no condition to be behind the wheel. After a few miles, I was pulled over by a white, female, law enforcement officer. She treated me perfectly reasonable and fair under the circumstances. I was properly arrested and without incident. Entering and being in the county jail for processing was a sobering experience for me. The following morning, I was bonded out of jail by my mother, and just in time to make it to the wedding. I spent the next several years living down the embarrassment, when paying the increased insurance rates caused by my DUI conviction.

Several years before my DUI, I had another encounter with the police while in my middle twenties, when an ex-girlfriend and I were pulled over while I was driving. I was a bit too drunk and high on weed. When the officer approached the car, it was after I had made a right turn into a gas station from the center lane. I was nervous as hell, but calm and respectful. I simply informed the officer that I was sorry, exhausted, and was only two blocks away from my destination. The officer lectured me, but then allowed me to drive the short remaining distance to my girl's apartment. Not only was I given a break, the officer probably should have performed a DUI investigation. There is no doubt that my calm demeanor with the officer, allowed me to be gifted the benefit of the doubt to avoid arrest. Driving drunk is stupid and extremely dangerous. Do not do it. I most certainly had to learn my lesson the hard way.

The last time a law enforcement officer was kind enough to give me a break, it was due to his discretion, and was during a very difficult time in my life. I was having health problems, family problems, and was generally angry and depressed. My mother and I have always had a close relationship, and if she were to call me or text me, I would most always return her message the same day. During that brief period of my life, I just went on what some folks call a "bender." I spent about two straight days drinking and smoking weed, slipping in and out from dozing off. Basically, I was in about a 24-hour blackout. As I awoke from my last grip of sleep, there was a loud banging on my apartment door. I was lying on the couch with a half empty pizza box. Stains were all over my shirt. Rattled and confused. I shouted, "Who is it?" The response was muffled, but I could tell that some kind of law enforcement official was at the door. Groggy and confused, I was not thinking about Fourth Amendment issues pertaining to why the police were there, or if they wanted to come in. I answered the door with a dry and pasty mouth. I was confused and curious as to why they would be banging on my door.

When I opened the door two officers stood before me. The one officer who was apparently in charge, informed me that my mother had requested a response to check on my well-being. Apparently over the previous couple days, if any of my friends had arrived at my door, I must have slept through it, or was in too much of a daze to answer. My mom sent 5.0. to see if I was alright! I quickly informed the officers that I was fine and apologized for any concern. Crucially, I remained calm and respectful, and this was even in my unkempt state. The officer just told me to call my mother as soon as possible. He must have repeated it about three times. Before I could close the door and put the puzzle pieces of my lost period together, the officer informed me that he saw my marijuana bowl and residue crumbs on my coffee table, but he was going to let it slide. My heart skipped a beat with the knowledge that the officer had clear probable cause to not only arrest me, but also search parts of my crib. I immediately thanked the officer with the utmost sincerity. Those two white law enforcement officers knew nothing about my drunk and stoned black ass, other than the fact there was a concerned mom somewhere. They decided to use their discretion to give me a break. I am eternally grateful.

The moral of this life-changing story--other than the fact that my beloved mom is very square and lacking in street smarts, by almost blowing up my spot--is the fact that there are good and compassionate law enforcement officials in this country. Also, there is no doubt that my demonstrated level of respect for their authority, played a part in their decisions to spare me entry into the criminal justice system. I am grateful for the officers' grace and compassion in letting the minor misdemeanor slide.

My ultimate message is, treat police officers with respect because this is the humane way to treat any professional. If you have the misfortune of encountering a demon cop, your composure and compliance can save you from being arrested, or from sudden death. Please keep a cool head. But, if you are ever mistreated by a law enforcement officer, and this is despite your compliance and calm demeanor, fight back only by exposing the situation. You do not have to be a victim of overbearing and oppressive law enforcement. Expose them and shame them. Believe that a large portion of American society is fed up with their demon cop ways. In this age of video recording and social media, along with the progress

For Black Men/Ali Shakoor

of our evolving standards of decency, this organic uprising against murderous cops and corrupt systems will continue to bring about positive change if we keep exposing misconduct. Be safe and preserve your black life at all times.

Chapter Six

Avoiding the Trap of Anger and Hostility

It is important to understand that there are people from many different cultures in American trying to address the problem of racism and economic bias in our communities. I discussed in a previous chapter how members in the white race put their lives on the line throughout the civil rights movement. So many whites are still trying to fight for justice today. I have been in meetings with these people, who range from young millennial folks to grandparents in their late seventies. Do not let your anger and resentment at white racism manifest itself into a hatred of all white people. That would be hypocritical and not productive.

I have a very diverse taste in music. I can appreciate most all genres, but classic rock and hip hop have the strongest hold of my heart. This does not mean I have not been to public establishments that play country music or metal. Whether I am a guest of a friend or simply in a bar which has a certain musical act playing on a certain night, I have been the minority in a place where I am literally the only, or only one of a very, very, few, black folks in the whole spot. There was one occasion where it took me a little too long to get service in some redneck bar, when I was in my twenties in Columbus, Ohio. The Confederate flag on the wall was a tell, that our race would not be kindly accepted. I walked out with a "fuck em" shrug. That is the only situation I can think of where I felt like white folks were openly discriminating against me or trying to make me feel unwelcome in a public establishment. And I have always gone out a lot; about two to three times a week. I am most often treated with respect by the white race when in alien surroundings, whether it be from the staff or other patrons.

Now I fully understand that does not mean I was not among any racists, but all I can go by is how I was treated. I also have no illusions that being the only black person in an establishment or area, does make it easier for white folks to hide any racist feelings, due to the lack of feeling threatened by my presence. Overt racism starts to really come into play when whites resent the number of blacks in their environment. I saw that in high school, as more urban blacks moved into my suburb. Another obvious example is when blacks left the dreaded south looking for freedom and opportunity in northern cities, only to find different, yet still very explicit forms of rejection and bigotry. Moreover, some of the same European countries who have rightly chastised America over the years for its "peculiar institution" and consistent mistreatment of black people, are now seeing their white citizens give a brutally cruel response to brown and black immigrants; particularly folks of Muslim origin.

But I digress. I am treated with courtesy and respect most of the times that I have ever been surrounded by white folks. This includes situations when I have been the obvious date of a white woman. No issues or negative treatment. During my short visits in their environments, courtesy and respect is all I ask for. Make me feel welcome and let's all have a great time for a few hours.

When I have taken or accompanied my white friends to events where our people are the majority, there have rarely ever been any problems. However, I can think of a couple unfortunate exceptions. One of my ex-girlfriends is white. She has been an advocate for equality and social justice all her life. I cannot think of a white person that I have encountered in my entire life that has been as entirely free of racial bias as her. She is not about paternalistic and condescending white guilt, as much as understanding institutional and structural racism, and living her life in opposition to such evil. She is genuinely good people.

We shared our first trip to New York City. Through work or vacations with friends and family, I had seen different parts of the country, but that was my first time finally heading to NYC. I was most certainly ready and excited about going to Harlem. Harlem has been regarded as the black capital of New York, and the namesake of the Harlem Renaissance. You too, may have read about or heard about the Harlem Renaissance. We had our talented and beautiful people like writers and thinkers: Langston Hughes and Zora Neal Hurston. Duke Ellington was one of the great composers and bandleaders of all time, and he thrived early in his career during the Harlem Renaissance. It was a place where many black folks migrated to, sought, and maintained a burst of creativity and accomplishments.

Remember watching Showtime at the Apollo? The Apollo Theater is iconic. Though built at the dawn of World War I, the Apollo Theater really became a hot bed of a crib for black talent in the 1930s and beyond. Vaudeville stand up acts, and particularly live music have found a home at the Apollo over the years. James Brown recorded his iconic album called *Live at the Apollo* in 1962. It is a special place.

Back to Showtime at the Apollo, most all of us watched it growing up, and for you younger folks, you can find the clips online. It was a proving ground for black talent: dancers, singers, and comediennes. Simon Cowell had nothing on the Apollo audience, when it came to judging talent in the most harsh and critical terms during Amateur Night. If you could not do your song justice by hitting the right notes, you would get mercilessly booed off the stage; prodded along by the house "Sandman," with his broom. And sheeeeeit, you could not try something ambitious like Jennifer Holiday or Whitney Houston, unless the vocal cord and control game were air tight. Countless popular musical artists would do guest spots on the show. Some, like Lauryn Hill, bravely made it through a live Amateur Night performance on their way to fame. The Apollo Theater has been an important cultural landmark for our people going on now for nearly 100 years. My girl and I were anxiously looking forward to visiting Harlem.

When we got off the subway and started walking into the heart of Harlem, I saw nothing but beautiful black people in every direction. I stood in front of the world-famous Apollo Theater and grinned, but unfortunately it was closed, and we were unable to get inside. We stopped inside a small shop. I was happy to patronize a black owned business in Harlem while buying some old Richard Pryor DVDs. However, what we felt during our walk through Harlem was unmistakable tension. There were some pleasant people, but they were easily equaled by the number of dirty looks. As I left one shop, a brother commented that I should not bring white girls into that part of Harlem. My girl told me that she had also ignored many derogatory comments directed at her during our walk. The bullshit we experienced was unacceptable. If there is anyone who should be tolerant and sensitive to "minorities" in our environment, it is black people. Like countless white people over the years in this country, she understands her privilege and has fought and sacrificed to help our people. She did not deserve such treatment.

On another occasion, this same ex-girlfriend and I were in West Palm Beach, Florida for a friend's wedding. During our extended stay, we decided to visit a hip hop club. The owner or manager of the club, a middle-aged white guy with a European accent that I could not place, was working the door with guys who looked and sounded like they were from the same part of the world. When we entered the club, the sound and vibe seemed just our speed and it did not matter to us that she was on the only white face in the spot. On our way to the bathroom, we absorbed ice glares from some of the patrons. After she got out of the lady's room, she was nearly in tears after explaining the race-based verbal abuse that was inflicted upon her. We knew it was time to call it a night and exit after a mere fifteen minutes or so in the joint. On our way to the door, I looked back, and she was just catching up to me as if she were held up by something. She told me that some asshole had pushed her in the back, knocking her to the floor, mocking her and telling her to get her white ass out the club. I angrily started glancing back into a sea of smoke and bodies looking for the culprit, as my girl smartly just pushed forward toward the exit. We told the guys working the door what we experienced, but we just received a shrug and smirk instead of our money back. Again, this is unacceptable behavior on the part of our people.

I am not a hypocrite. I have never treated white strangers in such a belligerent and disrespectful fashion. If you have, accept it as past errors in judgment that you can grow from. You have probably witnessed some of our people attempting to intimidate strangers who do not look likely to respond verbally or physically. How about the times our people will purposefully attempt to hold up traffic to finish a conversation at a disrespectful leisurely pace? Have you seen or displayed nastiness directed at service staff or customer support? Such conduct is a display of overflowing anger leaking out and it is the opposite of productive.

Dig it, racism is enraging. It can make you want to lash out and act ugly. But it's not an appropriate way to behave. When our anger manifests itself in such a fashion it is a grasp for some sense of power. The effects of institutional racism can be so devastating to the soul and psyche, you may want to respond with hatred and disgust. You may often want some sense of revenge.

You cannot take out your anger on someone just because they have the same skin color as many of our oppressors. That would be prejudiced. It is hypocritical. More to the point of his book, harboring such provocative hostility is bad for your soul and likely will cause you some serious problems. Refocus your emotions. You can rise and get "revenge" on your oppressors by being personally successful. There are few things that bigots hate more than a successful and talented black man. Refuse to be a stereotype that they can point to and mock with derision. It is just not emotionally healthy to be so nasty to complete strangers.

I am not asking you to be a punk or buster, who is supposed to always turn the other cheek when encountering some type of bigot or otherwise horrible person. I do not believe in "turning the other cheek." I find some things to be unforgivable. I would never forgive or show any semblance of respect or kindness to the likes of George Zimmerman or Mark Fuhrman, if I had the displeasure of encountering them. I would look at them as the wicked pieces of shit that they are and could recognize them as evil. On a more personal and direct level, if I know of someone to be a bigoted, I feel no desire to educate, or prove myself to them. Racists are evil and they should be swiftly dismissed. If the situation calls for it, our dignity may require a vigorous self-defense with words, or within the confines of the law, physicality. If you on the other hand, unlike me, are the forgiving sort, that is fine, too. Whatever it takes to suppress your desire to lash out in a provoking and violent way, is what you need to focus on.

The horrible situation I dealt with while protecting my sister and niece seemingly put my career in peril. Some of the people who had my back and wrote letters of support on my behalf, happened to be white and a few were staunch conservatives. Despite our many differences, we connected on a personal level as friends and shared mutual respect. Many whites are willing to put their reputations on the line for us, just like many whites have literally risked their lives in the fight for justice and equality. We cannot discriminate and generalize. I tend to like people. Most people are good. Do not let the comment sections of internet articles or the worst versions of humanity depicted on your television screens, cause you to be hateful against every perceived enemy.

I love Uber and Lyft. It is not just the convenience of getting to my destination safe and efficiently, but also due to some of the drivers I have encountered. I have met drivers of different ages and races. I have encountered white men and women who live in rural areas, driving to make extra money for their families. On a surface level we've had little in common. Hell, even beneath the surface, once you take political and religious views in account, we probably had very, very little in common. But digging deeper down inside, I have often found common ground and shared laughter. It could be about a favorite sports team or a new movie release. Maybe it's the joys of having nieces and nephews. We are all humans, most of us good, and it is so much easier to get along, at least on a temporary and superficial level. Take a chance to spend time with different races and ethnicities so that you can connect on a human level. Even if you encounter them by happenstance, be a gentleman.

Being respectful is not a sign of weakness. It is a demonstration of strength and self-confidence. Misplaced anger and unfocused aggression can lead you to a jail cell. Stand up for yourself and do not bow down when encountering disrespect but go into every initial situation as a man of dignity and kindness. I suppose my final piece of advice when coming into contact with someone who visually looks to be your complete opposite, and from a culture very different from your own, is just follow the "Golden Rule." To put it bluntly, don't be an asshole.

It should go without saying, the same goes for interactions with our own people. Most violent crime is perpetrated by someone close to you (family and friends), or by someone in your community who shares your racial or ethnic group. Yes, black anger and aggression is tragically misdirected at our own people. And, for what? We kill each other when committing robbery for money. We kill each other over drug territory. We kill each other for revenge and retaliation. Over women, and over slights big and small, we kill each other.

When I was in college at Ohio State, there was an annual event called the *Block Party*. It was essentially a bootleg version of Atlanta's old *Freaknik* event and was similarly hosted by black sororities and fraternities. Tens of thousands of our beautiful people would flood the streets of Columbus surrounding the campus area. Activities were spread out through the long weekend, such as step shows and small musical concerts. It was a great time for a young man digging the scene with my best buddies and our first true girlfriends. One night there was a large gathering outside of what must have been a few thousand people. The area was fenced off and filled with concession stands and lots of folks dancing. It was a great damn time. I walked away from my girlfriend to grab a drink at the concession stand. When I got my drink and turned to walk back toward my group, I heard screams and first witnessed an image that I would see a couple more times in my lifetime; a very large group of black people running in the same direction with frightened looks on their faces.

It was chaos. Everyone was running and screaming from the same location. I ran with the flow of traffic, and soon realized that my girlfriend and the group I was with were still inside. That was before cell phones. We are talking about the early nineties, here. Law enforcement was on the scene and I was unable to get back though the crowd. I made it back to the dorms and waited to reconnect with my girl. My fear and confusion turned to anger once I learned from others at the event that the reason why the whole mess started, is because one of our people pulled a gun on another brother. The reason why the gun was pulled and pointed is because a verbal dispute escalated after someone accidentally stepped on the other's shoe while walking through the heavy crowd. I have been near other incidents since then, where I have had to run with fear because one of our people pulled a gun.

I do not need to point you to statistics and lectures for you to understand that our people are harming and killing each other at startling rates, and for no good reason. When someone kills a fellow black person: they are taking another's loved one, families and communities grieve, certain far right conservatives with agendas feign concern while pointing and judging, racists mock us, and a victim has lost his or her precious life itself. As I stated in the opening chapter, the killing of another brother is most often accompanied by or later recounted with a description of the victim as a 'nigga.' It is shameful and must stop.

Though intra-racial violence is based on circumstances related to proximity and opportunity, our problems also involve self-hatred. We have learned from our oppressors for hundreds of years in this country to devalue ourselves. It is not a type of syndrome where black perpetrators feel a sense of loyalty and affection toward the white race. Rather, the hatred and anger are directed there as well; against all races, but conveniently, it is often directed at our own people in our own communities. Contrary to what certain types of conservatives tend to lie about, you know as well as I that there are nonstop efforts in our communities to get us to stop killing each other. It has often been a losing effort due to the way our government has destroyed the infrastructure in our communities coupled with the abysmal War on Drugs scheme.

But there has also been refusal by young brothers to value themselves and our people. Economic hardship is no excuse to be nihilistic. Life is not meaningless, and nor should your goals be selfish and shortsighted. Think about everything our people have been through and all of the sacrifices and struggles in this country. We are a resilient people, even greater and stronger than the sum of our parts. After coming over on the Middle Passage in chains and despair, followed by the horrors of slavery, and then Jim Crow, we still survived and rose. The next battle is reducing the cycle of intra-racial violence and becoming proactively in tune to fight the plague of mass incarceration. You can start by controlling your anger and self-hatred. We must stop killing ourselves in the name of vengeance, honor, greed and senselessness. Stop. Refocus your energy into self-improvement and fighting oppression.

For Black Men/Ali Shakoor

A large portion of violence occurs inside of the home, be it domestic violence or child abuse. Not only can the abuse of a child have a detrimental impact on his or her psychological development, it can cause you to lose custody and face criminal prosecution. I understand the confusing dilemmas in our community about trying to figure out good ole' fashion discipline versus abuse, or a whooping versus abuse, or popping a child in the face versus abuse, or feeling a need to inflict pain versus abuse, but we as black folks need to stop letting anger transition into physically harming our children. One of my ex-girlfriends had a little girl toddler during the time we were together. I was disheartened to see her lose her temper with the baby, who was no more than three, by popping her in the mouth for "back-talking" or threatening to pinch her for disobeying. She was otherwise a loving mother, but for those brief moments of tame sadism that she certainly must have learned from the elders in her family. Many of our people seem to think that children are property; and property that can be beaten and destroyed.

It is tragic to hit your child as if you would punch a wall or kick a chair over. It is devastating to curse a child in anger, as you want to do to your boss or landlord. Children are not inanimate objects or one of your possessions, or a reason for your despair. You are supposed to be their guardian and protector. Mold and teach them. There is also a sad misconception that the reason why our communities are in such bad shape, is because children are not severely beaten enough. Many black comediennes and elders peddle this pathetically inane concept. Besides the systematic discrimination we have talked about as imperiling our community, do not think for one second that the past two generations of young people caught up in the criminal justice system did not receive beatings in the home. We as black folks have never stopped beating our children. And it has never worked. This alleged African-American "Utopia" where our children stayed out of trouble due to a bunch of ass whoopings, never really existed. Beating your children will not help them deal with underfunded schools and racist teachers. It won't deter the police from harassing them or stop the flow of drugs into the community. It won't help you find an outsourced job. It won't keep you out of jail, but rather, it could make you more likely to become involved in the criminal justice system, yourself.

You may recall what kind of problems NFL great, Adrian Peterson, caused himself a few years ago. Peterson beat his then four-year-old son with what our community likes to call a "switch," a thin tree branch. What was this small child's crime, which caused Peterson to pull the small child's pants down bare-assed in front of onlookers as he beat the child to the extent to cause defensive wounds on the hands, along with bruises and lacerations on the legs, scrotum, back, and buttocks? The child allegedly pushed one of his

siblings off some kind of a toy.
http://houston.cbslocal.com/2014/09/12/exclusive-details-on-adrian-peterson-indictment-charges/

Peterson was temporarily suspended from the NFL for the incident and faced criminal prosecution before he was able to reach a plea deal arrangement which kept him out of jail. Fortunately, the probationary term kept him free of a felony conviction, and importantly, Peterson took advantage to attend counseling and parenting classes. He learned better ways to control his emotions and properly discipline his children. He should be proud of himself for evolving. My favorite legal phrase, *evolving standards of decency,* not only applies to broad and sweeping changes in the law, but also to one's personal conduct and morality. Just because we used to engage in certain conduct in the past, does not mean those practices should stand the test of time. Our culture, like the beautiful humans that fill it, grows and changes, while learning lessons and ways to improve itself along the way as a continuous work in progress.

Bitterness can negatively affect your self-esteem. It is very difficult being a black man in this country, if your past mistakes are hindering your future progress. You must also fight the challenges inflicted by systematic racism, which can make you feel like less of a man. This is tough. Life is tough. However, you cannot take out your frustrations by bullying people who are physically weaker. It is never acceptable to assault a woman.

Far too many of the men in our community put their hands-on women in a hostile manner. It's cowardly and detrimental. It is a matter of some men feeling like they need to dominate or control someone. So many aspects of life are beyond our control, certain men try to manipulate and dominate the other sex. A common pattern involves seeking out a woman with fragile self-esteem. Then the abuser figures out what the woman lacks in confidence about herself, and he finds a way to exploit that weakness. The abuser starts getting physical with the woman over issues and makes the woman think that the abuse is her fault. This is often done while the woman is either physically and/or emotionally isolated from her friends and family as a support system. Eventually, either because the woman gains the courage to turn the abuser in to the criminal justice system, or because the effects of the abuse are so tragically apparent, the abuser is eventually prosecuted. There are countless black men in prison for violence against women.

I have a younger cousin who has a permanent scar on her face due to being brutally beaten by her boyfriend. Apparently having a penchant for bad boys, she met and fell in love with a non-rehabilitated felon several years ago who had done time in prison. Every person with a negative past deserves the opportunity to showcase redemptive attributes and build a better life. Sometimes others want to take a chance with their own heart, and help another person bury the mistakes of their past and improve. That can be a beautiful thing. Nobody can accomplish their goals alone. Love, itself, also has its redemptive qualities. Unfortunately, not every man is good and ready to be redeemed. My cousin could have been killed.

With her young son asleep in the next room, an argument escalated to violence as the brutal man beat the shit out of my cousin. He twisted her foot and was successful in his attempt at breaking it. He picked up an iron, yes, an iron, and hit her upside the head with it, leaving a permanent scar. Throughout the attack, my cousin muffled her screams and tried her best to remain quiet, so as not to wake up her son. After the beating, the coward realized the damage that he had done and told my cousin to concoct a story about an intruder doing the damage to her. Fortunately, after the police and ambulance arrived, they could see through the weak attempts at cover. Since her father was a retired police officer, that helped spur on the culprit's arrest and prosecution. After failing to convince my cousin to not cooperate with the prosecution via manipulative letters, the coward entered a plea agreement for eight years in prison. Because this man was unable to control his anger and misogyny, he is going to spend most of the next decade requesting permission to use the bathroom, most often without privacy. He will be told when to wake up and when to go to bed. This man will not be able make love to a woman or enjoy wings at a sports bar while cheering on his favorite team. He is wasting an important time in his life, because of his hatred of women, which manifested itself into a brutal, awful, senseless attack.

Most all our men can point to a woman in their life who was instrumental as a positive influence in their upbringing. It could be a mother, grandmother, sister, foster mother, counselor, teacher, or a friend's mom who took a troubled young man into her home. No black man would want to see anything bad happen to the special women in their lives. We find it to be disgusting. Unacceptable. Yet, time and time again we see our brothers batter women and it is never justified. Some of you may be thinking of scenarios where women attack men, and the man should act in self-defense. Self-defense is a separate issue, and only necessary for the use of the most minimum means of force to protect one's self. Retaliation is not self-defense. Physically attacking a woman because of something she said, anything she has said, is not justified or self-defense. Deescalate and exercise self-control.

I think about my cousin's son and wonder if he was really sleeping. Other victims of domestic violence include the children who witness or hear the assaults. Did you hear about how Floyd Mayweather Jr's son, Koraun, called the legendary boxer a coward? http://www.usatoday.com/story/sports/boxing/2014/11/18/floyd-mayweather-josie-harris-domestic-abuse/19221605/ In September of 2010, Floyd, who already had several prior convictions for violence against women, viciously battered his ex-girlfriend and Koraun's mother, Josie Harris. He did this in front of Koraun and his siblings who were all crying and screaming. The best fighter of his generation was kicking and beating a woman, because she had moved on from their past relationship and was now dating a new man. This is the sense of ownership I discuss, as far as how some men feel about women. Brave Koraun, then only ten at the time, managed to escape from Floyd's goon who tried to stop him, as he ran for help. Young Koraun ran until he could get to a security guard in the building, who called the police to the scene to collect statements from Ms. Harris and the children. Floyd faced a stack of felony counts but managed to negotiate a plea agreement that resulted in a couple of months in jail. Koraun is right, his father was a coward for his despicable actions against a helpless woman. Young Koraun is a hero.

I wish I had his courage as a young child. Too many nights, I could hear my mother arguing with my monster of a stepfather. This always occurred while I was in my room, and my stepfather invariably came home drunk and high late at night. I could hear violence through the doors and walls but could never really determine what was going on. There were times when it sounded like he was smothering her with a pillow. As a child, this created a type of stomachache, which was not quite a pain and not quite nausea. It is hard to place the exact feeling, other than to call it extreme discomfort that was fueled by fear. It was the type of fear that made sleeping impossible until the violence stopped. Then the next day, I had to carry the shame, grogginess and fear with me throughout a day at school, or among my friends in the neighborhood.

One night, I finally gathered the nerve to call the 9-1-1, or 0 for the operator, I cannot recall what was used in that day. I just remember telling someone in a position of authority that my dad was hurting my mom. My stepfather did not get arrested that night. I just remember him coming into my bedroom and glaring at me in disappointment. After that night, the only other time I remember him attempting to get physical with my mom was during the period of the long overdue divorce proceedings, when they got in an argument over money as he was leaving the house. My mom slammed the door as he was leaving, and his finger was crunched in the process. He approached my mom to retaliate with a backhand, but I successfully intervened by grabbing his arm. He then left.

It is crucially important to understand the negative impact that domestic violence can have on children. Perhaps you also came from such a background, carrying fear and anger based on what you experienced. Break the cycle and set a good example, when it comes to self-control of your emotions.

For Black Men/Ali Shakoor

My stepfather was wicked. He hated women. He hated himself. He abused my mom and sexually abused my younger sister, his daughter, in particularly unconscionable ways. His name was Azeem Shakoor. He's now dead. You'll read more about his death, later.

Some of you reading this book have surely done some horrific things in your past. Some of these acts have caused you to suffer punishment through the criminal justice system, while other acts have resulted in dark secrets harbored between you and the victim. Or maybe the victim (s) is no longer around to talk. Regardless, in order to avoid a future of criminality, it is important for you to seek redemption. That starts with forgiving yourself. You cannot let your past failures weigh you down as if you are solely defined by what you did in your worst moments. I am reminded of one of my favorite scenes, in one of my favorite movies, *The Shawshank Redemption*. The character, Red, speaks to the parole board about how he has changed from the young man who committed the horrible crime that put him in prison for several decades:

"There's not a day goes by I don't feel regret. Not because I'm in here, or because you think I should. I look back on the way I was then, a young, stupid kid who committed that terrible crime. I wanna talk to him. I wanna try to talk some sense to him -- tell him the way

For Black Men/Ali Shakoor

things are. But I can't. That kid's long gone, and this old man is all that's left. I gotta live with that..."

Imagine what you would say to your younger self. You've been enlightened over the years about why and how you came to be. And of course, you're still searching, which is fine, because self-examination is an ongoing process. In chapter one, we discussed how *you* deserve a better life. Forgive yourself and realize that you deserve to be free from the sins of the past, free from perpetual anger and hatred.

There is no easy answer in figuring out the best way to deal with anger. For some, religion is the key to finding peace. Former heavyweight champion, Big George Foreman, was a surly and abusive man before dedicating himself to Christianity. Also, contrary to a great deal of rightwing propaganda, Islam can also offer a path to a peaceful mind. I am not a very religious person, but I can understand that for many people, a belief in a higher power helps bring meaning to lives. If a belief in a "God" helps you deal with anger and make a crime-free life more likely, and then go ahead with that route.

Just understand that you cannot pray away illnesses in the brain, any more than you can expect some type of spiritual entity to cure health problems like cancer and diabetes. Our people should do better about taking advantage of mental health treatment. It could be depression or a more serious type of psychosis, but it is extremely necessary for you to be honest with yourself about any possible illnesses and demonstrate the humility to seek help. It is not a sign of weakness, but rather a sign of immense strength to take your health seriously enough to address any mental health issues.

Another issue which may require some type of spiritual and/or professional intervention is substance abuse. People never set out to be strung out on drugs or alcohol. Addiction is what happens when your mind and body require continuous replenishment of a substance that can eventually kill you, after you have continuously tried to fix something inside of your mind by taking the substance. You cannot medicate yourself to address anger and sadness or a void. Addiction can get you wrapped up in the criminal justice system, when your ability to serve your needs is negatively impacted by a lack of funds to make the needed purchase.

The great Desmond Meade, the hero I discussed in a previous chapter for his ability to turn his life around, obtain a law degree and become an advocate for voting rights, spent time in prison because of crimes committed in service of his drug addiction. I cannot tell you how many clients I have had over the years, who have lost everything because of drugs. As I think of some of my current clients on death row in Florida, I can only shake my head at the thought of how their inability to control addiction issues caused them to commit capital crimes.

I think of my sweetest client, nicknamed Tree, because he is about 6'8" tall. His vice on the streets was powder cocaine. He and a codefendant committed a robbery, while high, to get some money for coke. Tree shot a lady during a carjacking while trying to escape the scene. There is no doubt in my mind that Tree would be a productive member of society, if he could have had the foresight to seek and take advantage of addiction counseling. He is just one of way too many examples. You can relate, or you have personally observed a similar tragic situation. It is necessary to take advantage of addiction counseling and treatment. Such services can literally save your life or the lives of others you may harm in pursuit of a fix.

This may be the most important chapter in the book because everything in life starts with self, and we are all controlled by how well we understand our emotional responses. I have never been angrier in my adult life than I was several years ago, when I was dealing with the fallout from my sister's case and George Zimmerman got away with killing Trayvon Martin. Despite what certain demographics like to say, it was never clear or proven that young Mr. Martin initiated the attack on the night of the killing. That story comes from George, himself. The case came down to reasonable doubt. Since some witnesses saw young Mr. Martin on top of George, and George's voice is heard yelling for help on the witness' 9-1-1 call, the jurors could not determine, *beyond a reasonable doubt*, that George was not acting in self-defense. That is it. That is why Zimmerman was acquitted. Honestly, all things considered and the way the state mishandled the case, it was a fair result. Nobody knows what happen before the physical altercation began. For all we know, George could have stuck a gun in the young man's face, and Mr. Martin punched him and took him down in self-defense to save his own life. George is the one who had a history of prior arrests before the murder, and then more arrests after the acquittal. Yet, certain demographics would rather call young Mr. Martin the thug. They can call me a thug, too, because I was a teenager who drank, used drugs, got into fights and other troubled teenager shit. And if some creepy piece of trash was following me home while I walked alone, I would do my best to defend myself if threatened. Fact is, if George simply reported his *concerns* to law enforcement and had them come out to investigate, young Mr. Martin would be alive today, as he was simply walking home from the store, on a rainy night, while talking on the phone with his friend. Regardless, George Zimmerman was and will always be a hero to certain demographics, and young Mr. Martin the so-called "thug."

When it comes down to character and credibility, there are two witnesses to what led to the altercation that night. One was a seventeen-year-old boy who was shot in the heart and killed, so he cannot tell the story. The other is alive, in his mid-thirties, is periodically getting arrested, and called various black people "apes" on Twitter, before he was kicked off Twitter for posting private nude pictures of an ex-girlfriend, who George wrote, cheated with a "dirty Muslim." George also regularly calls our people "niggers," and those who defend us, "nigger-lovers." He draws pictures of the Confederate flag and sells them. He mockingly advertised and sold the gun he shot Trayvon Martin with. The piece of shit also signs bags of Skittles for his many fans. That's George, for you. We have not heard the last of him, either. He enjoys this form of mocking and taunting. But he will always be a hero to racists and/or others with certain perspectives on the "conservative" end of the spectrum. I believe Zimmerman is pure evil.

The murder of Trayvon Martin had a profound effect on me. It was enraging. I fumed and purged Facebook "friends." However, I had a revelation to turn my anger into positive action. I decided to get involved as a big brother in the Big Brother's Big Sister's program. I wanted to use some of my free time to help young black males navigate through dangerous waters and bigots with guns. Though my volunteering experiences, I became acquainted with The Boys and Girls Club of America, a wonderful organization that positively provides safety and guidance for youth outside of school.

Occasionally, throughout the year I spoke to young teenagers at a predominantly black Boys and Girls Club in Tampa, so I could offer some advice and guidance about a lot of the same issues I touch on in this book; particularly encounters with law enforcement.

As I touched on in a previous chapter, I am also now more active in my community for causes related to social justice and fighting oppression. I have met some very inspiring people along the way. Being active in improving the community helps to alleviate the power of helplessness in the face of oppression, and of course this sense of helplessness fuels the anger. I decided to write this book. I am telling you to take your anger, examine the reason for it, and try to fight for better opportunities for our people. Be more productive by engaging in positive factors that you can control. Stay engaged. Get active. Write down your thoughts and concerns as a form of venting. Maybe even write a book. Just don't let your anger continue to negatively affect your life. Take control.

Chapter Seven

Education and Career Choices

Unless you are elderly or severely handicapped, every healthy adult American man needs a job. This is not a choice. It is essential. In order to stay out of the criminal justice system, you must dedicate yourself to some type of career path, which is something to cultivate and cherish. Obviously, we need money to survive in this country. The key is to obtain it by legal means. I fully understand how in certain communities the absence of employment has left our people with drug dealing as the source of income. It is about demand and supply. The government fails to prevent the shipments of drugs entering our communities, creating widespread demand due to addictions. Drug dealers then supply the product. Drug dealing can be lucrative, but only for the folks at the top, the folks who do not live in your community. Nah, at the local level, in the streets, you know it really is not very lucrative at all. It puts some money in your pocket for basic needs or minor extravaganzas. Maybe it helps you pay bills or those of a loved one. That sounds all fine and good, but the standard perks of a typical job are sorely lacking. This type of "employment" does not come with health benefits or a retirement plan. It is usually short-term. The job is hazardous to the point of being life threatening to not only yourself, but perhaps those close to you. Another obvious point in fact, is that it is illegal. The draconian drug laws are designed to feed you to the prison industrial complex where you waste your life away until and unless you are ever released. There are better and more productive ways to make a living.

One benefit, yes, "benefit" is the word I am using, of the drug trade, is that once you exit the life, there are tools that you can apply to legitimate work. You ever check out the documentary *American Gangster*, narrated by actor, Ving Rhames? It's a series which aired on BET, and most of the episodes focused on a black American drug dealer from the past who rose from poverty to the top of the drug game; usually becoming a multimillionaire. Like any stories about a big-time drug kingpin, they served as cautionary tales, because drug dealing will inevitably lead to imprisonment or death, if you don't get out of the game in time. Of course, any current or recent drug dealers reading this book are looking to exit the business.

Anyway, the *American Gangster* franchise demonstrated the brilliance of our people as businessmen. With minimal education, these men were able to create multimillion-dollar businesses, with international ties and multiple levels of management. Do you know what type of intelligence it takes to handle distribution, accounting, payroll and orders? These men often engaged in and prevented takeovers from competitors, and sometimes brokered merger agreements.

Imagine if such talents could have been used for legitimate legal purposes. Even with the understanding of how systemic racism makes it difficult for our people to secure loans and grow businesses, difficult, does not mean impossible. There are black owned businesses all over the country. If you've been engaging in the drug dealing game, I am telling you once again to forgive yourself and learn from your past mistakes. Get out while you are alive and free. Importantly, take your talents in discipline and hustle and transfer those skills to the legitimate side of life, like Jay Z did. I am not even saying you should become a businessman, let alone a mogul, but you can still use the skills you possess to be hard worker and model employee. Just redirect your brilliance.

Entry into the work force requires an educational foundation. Take advantage of the free compulsory education you started receiving as a small boy. Complete the basics, if you have not done so already. Learn a trade, either in a private apprenticeship or at a vocational school. College is not for everyone, but if you are so inclined, take the next step in pursuit of a college degree.

I almost never went to college. Oh, I will certainly explain.

Recall earlier in this book, I told you about how my mother made sure our family always lived in a good school district. No matter how bad things were at home with the horrors of domestic abuse, and regardless of the job market as we moved all around Central Ohio, my mother always made sure we resided in a top-level school system. She understood the importance of education from my grandparents and through her own sense of black empowerment. From towards the end of my fifth-grade year until high school graduation, we resided in Worthington, Ohio, the suburb I described earlier where I often felt like Malcolm's "mascot."

I was not the only black kid in the school, but there were very few of us. My best friend to this day, Chris, was in my grade, and there were a few of us sprinkled across every class in every grade. However, for example, I still look at my seventh and eighth grade basketball team photos every time I visit my mom's house. I am the only black guy on the entire basketball team. This is basketball, I am talking about. Basketball! Anyway, after my mom divorced my sadistic stepfather while I was in junior high, and then following my soaking in Malcolm's memoirs during my freshman year, I was beginning to change on the inside.

Obviously, this is the period of hormonal changes and brain development that is crucial in the makeup of every human, but I was also starting to feel even more like an outsider in my own little ecosystem. I had a small circle of varied race friends, feeling closest to the black ones, and I was a good student rocking the A's and B's, and only the occasional C. I was also a solid athlete--good in both basketball and track--which further insured my popularity. I was not in the main in-crowd, which was generally based on socioeconomic status, but I was popular enough and had good acquaintances across different social groups. I was not good with girls at the time; skinny and woefully lacking in game and confidence.

My existence as a minority, with the DNA and planted seeds toward black consciousness, along with the demons from a turbulent home life created a bubbling of confusion and a lack of comfort in my own skin. I started getting in trouble at school a little bit during the period of seventh grade through ninth grade. I engaged in mild bullying and got in fights. I was a fist-fighter who threw more looping right hooks for minor transgressions during that period of my life, than the rest of my life combined. Recall I first read the life-changing *Autobiography of Malcolm X* while sitting at in-school suspension during the ninth grade.

Right before I turned sixteen, a traumatic event occurred in my life. My best friend, mentor, hero, beloved grandfather died of cancer at the tragically young age of fifty-nine. That was a devastating blow, as the whore of a disease entered his body in such a rapid and continuous way, it seemed that I could hardly process the grave diagnosis by the time that I found out he was literally on his deathbed. Months sped as he wholly declined. I remember rushing down the hospital hall and quickly brushing past my grandmother's embrace, and by the time I got to his body, he was gone. It was the first and only time that I ever touched a dead body. He was gone. Just a cold and clammy shell remained, of what was once a robust and sturdy embodiment of black American manhood.

The funeral was fascinating in the sense that although my grandfather was a fixture of my entire existence up until that point, I met Andrew L. Jordan for the first time. Although I knew he was a high school teacher and I had been to his classroom many times during my life, I was still seeing him during those school visits in the context as my grandfather. Andrew L. Jordan, on the other hand, was a beloved teacher to grieving students and colleague of coworkers dripping in melancholy. As the oldest grandchild, I held it together strong and tough for the family as far as composure is concerned, until one of those colleagues, an older white man, began telling sweet-hearted stories about how my grandfather raised five girls and was looking forward to having a grandson to do "manly" stuff with, such as fishing and hunting. I lost it at that point.

After my grandfather's death, another change started happening in my school life. The district boundary lines seemed to expand a little bit, and more black kids arrived. Others moved in. At the time, I existed in my tight little black trio from age 12, which consisted of me, Chris, and our buddy Claude. Chris and Claude were middle-class kids from two-parent homes. We were like brothers, sleeping at each other's cribs many weekends and all falling in love with the wonderful American art form known as rap music. Outside of the circle, but often mixing with us, there were a few other middle-class blacks. Most all of them, unlike me at the time, were from financially stable two-parent households. Perhaps that's why I felt like an outsider, even among us.

I began to seek out something else. No, "seek out" may not be the right term, but maybe I should state *accept* that I had less in common with them. Besides my love for rap music, I was also developing a love for classic rock music. I was a music bigot until the point where I discovered the great rock music of the '60s and '70s; I stubbornly sustained myself on rap music, black pop artists and my beloved Motown sounds. I fell in love with classic rock while working in a pizzeria, which was my second or third job at the time. I have been working every year since I started making $3.55 an hour as a fourteen-year-old at Burger King. Anyway, while gigging at this pizzeria around the time of my sophomore year, the radio station in the kitchen was always on the classic rock station. I just fell in love with the music and was always asking a white dude who the artists were. I began my own research into the music, just as I had previously done with my black sounds. It started with Bob Dylan, who will always hold a special place in my heart, along with the Rolling Stones. There are so many great songs and fascinating artists.

I also came to understand the relationship between the music and the civil rights movement which I already had a foundation in. It all just fit. I had my own thing. I was starting to understand myself and would spend hours alone in my bedroom reading and listening to records and cassette tapes. I could feel myself drifting apart from my clique. The love was still there, it's just that I was exploring myself in this new individualized escapism of reading about and listening about peace, love, sex, drugs and music. At this point in my life around '92-'93, I was pretty much mostly listening to rock music and rap, which was soon regularly being referred to as hip hop.

I was not always alone, however. A couple of the brothas I was hanging out with, who were new to me in Worthington, also worked at the same pizzeria. Reggie and Tommy, both a year ahead of me, became my new friends and running crew. It happened organically. All three of us came from somewhat dysfunctional home lives. Although I was relatively square at the time, and they were more "street" and well versed in the ways of getting laid, we all just clicked. We became tight and started hanging. I would still hang out with Chris and Claude on occasion and they were still my "fam," so to speak, but I was definitely growing away from them. Plus, they were good with girls, had lost their virginity and were just living what I interpreted as the ideal black suburban existence. I did not fit in with that, in my mind at the time. Chris and Claude had game with the black girls. I loved the sistas, but they would not give me the time.

Reggie and Tommy rolled with the white girls. The white girls were giving me some holla, and my horny ass wasn't one to discriminate. I have been horny all my life. I never went through that stage where boys thought girls had the "cooties" or some shit. I remember having crushes on my preschool teachers, along with wanting to be with different girls and teachers at each grade level in development. Erotic programming on late night premium cable was also an escape. I have always loved women and literally everything associated with sex. I just felt left out. I had a kiss here and there, and a so-called girlfriend or two, but I never had the confidence to really hold down a good friendship and seduction game. I could not close the deal to hit it.

As I write these thoughts down, this could be a good time to take a quick break to apologize to some of my girlfriends and beneficial friends in my adult life, even leading up to most recent times, for my restless spirit and commitment-phobe nature- always wondering what else is out there. I suppose I have been making up for what the former young teen Ali lacked in terms of confidence, game and sheer numbers. As I approach fifty and see myself having purposefully and happily avoided the wife and kids existence of my peer group, with comfort in my sense of self, and having indulged every erotic fantasy that I have ever had, I can say that I will settle down someday soon. It has taken me up until now, to understand these things about myself. Anyway, I digress.

Also, unlike Chris, Claude and the rest of the middle-class Worthington square blacks that I had associated with, I knew Reggie and Tommy liked to drink and get high. I was slow to it at first as they took me under their wing. I know a lot of teens typically have their first drink way earlier than I ever even thought to try. I did not have my first drink until I was seventeen years old. It was some cheap 42 proof convenience store vodka mixed with juice. I loved the feeling instantly. I lost my virginity with a white girl that same night. This all happen in the darkness of my boy Reggie's basement. It was me, Reggie, Tommy, Tommy's cousin, and two white girls. I was lying down on the basement floor, and this hot redhead plopped on top of me and started making out. I wanted to be able to see what was going on, and find a condom, so I led her to the basement bathroom. After I busted in minutes, the girl I was with left me and moved on to Tommy and his cousin who started to double team her in the corner of the basement. Reggie was banging out the other white girl during this time, as I passed out into a content sleep on the basement bathroom floor.

No doubt in my present feminist mind, that it was all consensual. I'm not ashamed nor proud of my first experience. That's just the way it was back then. That's how it all started for me, and how I lived the rest of my junior year through graduation. That was me and the crew. Our lives consisted of basketball, alcohol, weed, and always hooking up with white girls. Classic rock was still my own private thing. Biggie, Nas, Dre and Snoop were part the soundtrack to my life with the crew. Those days were a foundational period in my life. I am not a religious man at all, but there is a quote attributed to my favorite male vocalist, Marvin Gaye, that I read in a biography on his life, *Divided Soul*, as he said about himself regarding an early sexual experience:

"...understanding that in my life the pleasures of the devil were going to give the joys of God some mighty stiff competition."

Yeah man, I felt the same way as I was having the time of my life, while still feeling a void inside of myself.

Obviously, my grades dropped during this time. The classes I was interested in, such as the social sciences, English/literature, and theater, I did well. However, I took an "L," failing chemistry and Algebra 2. I quit playing basketball for the school, instead enjoying the pressure-free intramural league. After lettering in track as a captain and damn good 400-meter runner as a junior, my defiance and "locker-room lawyer" mentality caused me to be stripped of my captainship as a senior before I quit the team to spend more time partying with my friends and working at Toys R Us. Reggie and Tommy both graduated ahead of me, but they were still my homies thru and thru. Reggie spent some time in a juvenile center for his part in a robbery of the pizzeria where we used to work. Tommy was in a nihilistic mode after losing his mom to cancer and began selling dope. My illegal activity during this time was underage drinking, truancy, occasional petit theft and getting high on weed.

My fascination with rock'n roll drug culture did inspire me to take an ill-fated trip on acid during my senior year. That was an embarrassing disaster. I was at a party with the crew, drinking cheap vodka and I decided to finally take a psychedelic surf like my man Jimi Hendrix and many others did back in the day. I bought one dose for about $5.00. I did not feel anything for quite a while and then it hit me. The otherworldly feeling was interesting at first and definitely something like I could not even imagine. But after a few hours, enough was enough. I am thinking, "Cool, I'm good. I'm done"

Acid wasn't done showing me what was what.

I remember this was a Friday night, because I had Saturday school the next day for some transgression that I cannot recall. As the party was winding down, I figured I would go home and sleep it off. Nope. I was up all night seeing distorted images around my room and having this continuous vision of cartoon characters on a conveyer belt; about five rows on top of each other of cartoony animals in neon colors going left to right, over and over and over. I saw that crazy shit every time I closed my eyes.

The next morning after a night alone in my room and avoiding my mom and sister, I drove myself to Saturday school. My buddy Adrian was also there. I probably should have mentioned Adrian earlier, as we had been pretty tight since junior high. We were in the same grade. Adrian moved in to Worthington from a city school with is mom, stepdad and little brother. He was a funny dude, short and skinny, with a personality that reminds you of a young Chris Rock. I was close with him and he spent a lot of time kicking it with me, Chris and Claude. Those three hours in Saturday school felt like a semester. I had gas and trouble sitting still. Paranoia and lack of sleep were controlling my mind, along with distorted images all over the room where I felt like different students were staring me down. It was nightmarish. It was just a horrific feeling.

Once Saturday school was over, I carefully drove Adrian and I back over to the same party I was at the night before, so I could inquire about the acid I took. The crib was a house where a lot of druggie kids from the area hung out at and was shared by White Boy Jay and his mom. In retrospect, White Boy Jay's mom was probably a meth head. Teenagers were always staying over and coming and going at all times. A couple of dudes were banging the mom on occasion. Anyway, when Adrian and I got to the drug house, folks were just lying around passed out. I did not feel any more comfortable there, and Adrian certainly was not feeling the vibes, so we left after about twenty minutes. By the time we left White Boy Jay's crib, I came to the long tardy conclusion that I was not fit to drive. I gave Adrian the keys to the 1987 Isuzu Pup that I inherited from my grandfather and tried to figure out my next plan.

Just as we were leaving, a cop pulled up before we could drive away. He informed us about the house being under investigation for possessing stolen property obtained from burglaries in the Worthington area. We didn't even have to play dumb, because neither of us knew anything about it. I gave a lie about only going to the house to retrieve a jacket I had mistakenly left there the night before, after accompanying some friends to this place I did not know who or what about. The cop left and Adrian drove home to his house, where I left him. I spent the rest of the day visiting friends and trying to figure out how to tell my mom that I had foolishly given myself permanent brain damage.

By the early evening and still tripping balls, I was growing paranoid and hysterical with panic. I decided to drive myself to the hospital to see if any damage could be undone. Through my tears and rambling, I was directed to the proper unit where the staff calmed me down. They told me that I had to call my mom.

During this time from my junior to senior year while I was finding these new friends and creating a new version of myself, mom was holding it down as a hardworking single parent of two teenage kids. My sister was excelling in school while quietly dealing with the effects of what her dad had done to her. I was very good at hiding my frequent drunk and high state from them. Needing dough, I was diligent about keeping my part-time job at Toys R Us. Every morning, I drove off to school and tried to maintain. Naturally smart when it comes to things I am interested in pursuing, I did well in some classes, while bombing others. I simply quit going to Chemistry class. The old Chemistry teacher surely did not seem to care. He never reported me. Since Reggie and Tommy had already graduated, I drifted amongst various cliques including druggie white chicks, Adrian and Chris whom I was still casually cool with, and even a few theater hipsters. I loved acting. I played intramural basketball. I kept busy. Mom really had no reason to know my life was becoming unraveled.

If I was loaded, I kept a low profile, feigned teenage exhaustion, and retreated to my room. The only time I would drink at home was occasionally during lunch, when I would go to a local convenience store that reliably sold tall boys to underage folks. I threw one house party while my mom and sister visited my grandma in Toledo. It was not too crazy of an event or anything. The dude to girl ratio was way unbalanced, but it was a decent time. I was careful to keep things tame. I respected mom's house and did not want any drama.

But that drama nearly came in the form of a head being blown off when Deleon came through with his crew. Deleon was a short and stocky brother, built like a human battery-tough as hell reputation. He also moved in from the city schools. The clique he ran made me, Reggie, and Tommy look like Theo Huxtable and friends. They liked to go find drunken fights to get into and often spent their nights breaking into cars. I was growing concerned that Adrian was starting to spend so much time with them. As the party was winding down, Tommy was crashed out on the couch. Deleon drunkenly pulled out his .45 and pointed it at Tommy's head while rambling something about some beef. We all grew dream-state silent. Tommy woke up freaked out, and then Deleon just started laughing as he put his gun away. I am glad I did not have to figure out a way to explain a murder in the first home my mother ever bought for us.

For Black Men/Ali Shakoor

Well, there I was in the "crisis center" type section of this hospital with the phone in my hand and telling the nurse the number to my mom's house. When she answered the phone, I think my first words were "I'm at a hospital, I took acid, and I think I'm going to die." My heart skipped a beat as my mom freaked out, "Whawhaaattt you go and do something like that for?!?!!!!"

I cannot recall what immediately transpired after that. My mom was in the middle of relaxing my sister's hair and relayed my details to her. My sister got on the phone crying, "Why do you want to die, why didn't you tell me you were so sad???" Geesh, my embarrassment was now compounded by the fact that my family thought my hellish acid trip was a suicide attempt. I plopped down in a bed and waited for my mom to come and pick me up. Thankfully, about twenty hours into my first LSD experience, I was starting to feel like I was finally leaving my high.

The ride home with my mom was certainly awkward, but she was very understanding about everything I had been through. Sleep deprivation and acid residue had me in confessional mode talking about feeling uncomfortable in my skin and experimenting with the darker side of life. As I walked up the stairs headed for a long period of deep sleep, I stopped and saw that my mom had already framed my senior photograph. I looked handsome and healthy in the picture. I did not recognize myself at all.

Eventually I missed my buddies and girls and partying, and slowly sank back into the life after a couple weeks or so. I just avoided LSD. As my senior year was coming to an end, I came to a nerve-wrecking realization. My slacking off and failures put me at risk of not graduating if I did not handle business. Thankfully, I managed to pass. As I saw some of my classmates graduate with honors and excellence, I barely made it with about one and a half credits to spare.

I hated high school. I hated waking up early and hated the structure. I hated being forced to take subjects I had no interest in. It was a bad fit for me. In retrospect, there were a couple options I should have pursued instead. By best friend Chris, whom I had grown apart from, while maintaining the love, went to something called the Fort Hayes Career Center. He struggled with academics and at some point, his family and guidance counselors discovered this option, which allowed him to have Worthington as a home school for sports and whatnot. But Fort Hayes was in the city and had less structure, more individual attention, and more subject options; in his case radio and television. Chris thrived at Fort Hayes and eventually went to college and earned a degree. Another option I could have pursued was the Linworth Alternative School. A lot of burnouts, art-fucks, and general outsiders went there. Frankly, that's what I was and where I probably belonged. My point is that there is more than one way to learn and grow, when it comes to educational development. Keep that in mind as you pursue your own educational or vocational goals. Explore your options and find the right fit.

Oh yeah, college. Nah, I did not plan on going, at least not right away. I understood how important a college education was in my family and figured I would get to it eventually, just not right away. My mother dropped out of college after she had me as a freshman, before getting back to her degree later in life. College would always be an option for me, I figured. I wanted to take a year or so to move in with Reggie and Tommy, or maybe get my own crib, hold a job, and party. I ignored my mom's requests to apply for any schools and just worked the summer after my graduation. Halfway through the summer, I had a change of heart after my mom told me that she filled out an application for me to attend The Ohio State University and I was accepted to start that fall. My grades were too mediocre for scholarships, but I did qualify for income-based grants, loans, and the work-study program. Acceptance changed my perception. My only insistence was that I wanted to move out into the dorms. I loved my mom and sister, but I had a thirst for freedom.

Living with Reggie and Tommy was never a realistic option, anyway. Though I was a weed smoker and drinker, their drug-dealing ways--including crack--did not sit right with me. It was just not my scene. I liked to dabble in the urban criminal life, but I was also bred with undeniable bourgeoisie tendencies. I did not really feel relaxed or comfortable in any environment, as "Bobby Dupea" from *Five Easy Pieces* and "Preach" from *Cooley High*, had been the American characters that I related to for the overwhelming majority of my life, and up until recent times.

I spent the summer before my start in college just finishing up at Toys R Us, and partying with my boys for the last time before school started. In retrospect, I think that was the obvious fork in the road in my relationship with these dear friends of mine. We still kicked it, but not as often and we seemed to acknowledge our disparate immediate career paths. I was planning on going to college. They were going to sell dope and hustle for a while.

In September of 1993, I moved into Baker Hall on the South Oval at the Ohio State University. I was the only brotha in my hallway and I had a white roommate from a small town named Greg. Eventually, I befriended a white dude across the hall named Chad, and he traded places with Greg as my new roommate. There was another white dude named Jason I ran into on campus by happenstance. Jason was a childhood buddy that I used to play basketball with, who transferred to a different suburbia towards the end of junior high. We reconnected and became fast friends once again, sharing a common interest in girls, alcohol and sports. My Worthington upbringing had already prepared me for life as a minority surrounded by white students. But I still found my sense of culture. I started spending time at the Black Cultural Center at Ohio State, and eventually had my work-study assignment transferred there.

I still hung out with my old homies from Worthington on occasion, too. I did well in school. College life suited my laid-back attitude about school as far as only taking the classes that I was interested in and attending when I wanted to. I maintained a B to B+ average throughout college while going to school year-round, often carrying twenty credit hours at a time and working. I was also maintaining my first serious relationship with a sista named Dana.

My goal was to finish college as quickly as possible. I always viewed school as a means to an end. During college, I decided that I wanted to attend law school. The social science type classes appealed to me the most, as I majored in Political Science with minors in Black Studies and Women's studies. There was not much I felt I could do with those types of degrees, other than go into teaching— something I should have strongly considered in retrospect—but law always appealed to me. Plus, like most of the nation, I was heavily addicted to the O.J. Simpson trial. Becoming a lawyer also allowed me to showcase my interests and talents in debate, theater, research, and pursing justice.

In June of 1996, less than three years after I started, I graduated from the Ohio State University with about a B+ average. I was accepted into and ready to start at Ohio State's law school in the fall. I was twenty-one years old and everything should have been in place for my future, but something was missing. My college girlfriend and I had broken up at this point, but random sex wasn't too hard to find. In retrospect, I think I was starting a period of severe depression, coupled with an unsettled identity I carried with me for a good portion of my life. If I could talk to that version of myself or build a time-machine, I would put that version of Ali in counseling. That would be counseling to deal with leftover childhood issues and a feeling of being lost. I had made my choice not to go down the road of Reggie and Tommy, but what was I left with? The world of academia and square folks did not feel like it was for me, either.

So, what about Reggie and Tommy? Reggie was slinging dope during that time and struggling with a bourgeoning cocaine habit. Tommy, I remember the last time I saw Tommy as a free man.

I was out one night, lonely with a buzz, and ran into Tommy at the Burger King on High Street. That Burger King parking lot was always a cool hangout spot on the college campus during that period. Hip hop and young black folks enjoying each other, was what it was all about. There was never really any drama, either. Cool spot. So, one night I left my campus apartment bored and alone and swung by

Burger King. I ran into Tommy for the first time in what seemed like a grip. We dapped up and caught up on what we'd been missing out on in each other's lives. The differences in career paths were stark. I was on my way to becoming a lawyer and Tommy was still working part-time and slinging full-time. We didn't have much in common other than shared love and memories.

For old time's sake, we decided to cruise the campus streets together and see if we could run into some ladies. Me, anal about being towed, wanted Tommy to follow me to my crib and leave my car, just a few blocks away. Tommy thought I was being ridiculous and tried to assure me that my car would be safe in the Burger King parking lot. Finally relenting, Tommy agreed to follow me. As I looked in the rearview mirror after I crossed the intersection, I saw Tommy turn down the street on his way. Pissed and lightweight hurt, "fuck Tommy," I thought. Of course, I had no idea at the time that would be the last time I'd ever see Tommy as a free man.

A while later, I received word from Reggie that Tommy had gone to trial and been convicted for Aggravated Murder and Attempted Aggravated Murder. He was sentenced to thirty-nine years to life in prison. He's not eligible for parole till 2035. He got into a dispute with some strangers inside a north side club that we used to kick it at. The beef continued into the parking lot, and the argument escalated into predictable and unnecessary gun violence, as

For Black Men/Ali Shakoor

the bullet from Tommy's heater hit one young man, who was apparently firing at Tommy, and while another bullet killed a brother on the opposing side. Just like when Reggie was the getaway driver during the robbery of the pizzeria we used to work at, I am so fortunate that I was not there.

My first year of law school at the Ohio State University was a horrible and lonely time. In retrospect, I was probably clinically depressed. I started out okay and was dating a Taiwanese graduate student for a little while. Eventually she relocated for a job in Los Angeles, and I was in a school I had no interest in being at anymore. I was burnt out and lonely. It was a mistake to rush through undergrad so fast. I didn't allow myself to enjoy the college experience and date around more. God, I hated law school. I rarely went to class and I was drinking almost every night. When I did go to class, I would often sit in the back row all by myself with a hoodie like some type of brooding weirdo. I started spending more time with Reggie and other folks who allowed me to indulge in booze, drugs and sex. I recall my mom attempting an intervention, and I did rally to at least attend final exams, but by the end of the year, I had pitifully flunked out. The summer after that year I made the effort to petition a committee to let me back in school, which worked. However, I barely made it through the fall term before I simply decided to drop out of law school.

My family was disappointed, but I was relieved. I was tired of school and bored with bourgeoisie intellectuals. I was going to keep working until I decided what I wanted to do. That is one important detail to keep in mind- I always worked. During the first year of law school, 1Ls are not allowed to work, but I worked during other parts of the year, and every year since my first job at Burger King as a fourteen-year-old making $3.55 per hour.

I also wanted to pursue my passion for acting. I didn't have the balls to go the "starving artist" route in L.A. or New York, so I got a local Columbus, Ohio based agent and went on auditions all over the Midwest. I didn't get much work beyond a local play, a low budget commercial, and a film shot on location at Ohio State, which was never released. Through it all, I enjoyed the experience. For money, I did a lot of temp work. I also had such strange gigs as working at a karaoke distribution center and selling home security systems. I just wanted enough money to pay my bills and party.

Those were truly some decadent years for me in the late nineties. I spent more time kicking it with Reggie (always asking when I would go back to law school) and other friends who liked to party. Besides weed and liquor, my drug intake included experimenting with cocaine a few times; thank goodness I never liked it. Being dumb and competitive, I decided to try LSD a couple more times and those episodes went just fine.

I also had another close run-in with a potential life-changing legal situation. In the fall of 1998, I was working part-time selling electronics for commission at Sears while trying to get my modeling and acting moves on. The gig was less than two miles from my apartment. Sometimes during my lunch break, I'd go hang out with my upstairs neighbors; an urban oriented white dude, his older sister, and various characters that frequented the spot. I only smoked with them during my off hours, because I was usually too paranoid to be high at work. One day while heading home from work I saw a huge, imposing, police presence around the crib. I peeped my neighbor friend cuffed over a cruiser. Needless to say, I drove right past them. I later found out that the cops had rammed the door in and made several arrests for stolen property and drugs in their crib. As I often heard alluded to on occasions while visiting, my upstairs neighbors would sometimes engage in home invasions around town. If I had been there a mere thirty minutes earlier, I would have been caught up in some really heavy stuff.

My life took an interesting turn as I approached the end of the century. I was still working temp jobs and trying to figure out something more permanent. Through a connection with an older friend from Worthington, I applied for and got a job with a real estate development company. It was a great gig for a young single guy. Basically, this company would send me all over the country to do market research and help determine whether there was a good place to build apartment complexes or commercial real estate. The salary was very decent for a single person, and I got a per diem while on the road. It is crucially important to note that I never would have been offered the position, if I did not have a four-year college degree.

Man, I was all over this great country. They sent me to so many interesting places, including: Miami, Philly, Las Vegas, what was left of Detroit, Tucson, and Nogales, Arizona, which allowed me to cross the border into Mexico for the first time. I went to Los Angeles and positively fell in love with the city. Really, I am totally into the landscape and vibe in the Pacific Southwest of the United States. Maybe I'll look to retire out there someday.

I went to a Native American reservation in South Dakota, which was basically a small village. Once I got off the plane at the tiny Bismarck, North Dakota airport and started my adventure to the job site, I grew concerned that I would not be able to find a hotel within an hour of where I was working. Frankly, I was always also hoping to run into some type of adventure with a lady while on the road, too. I drove and saw parts of America that I could never imagine seeing, like plains of nothingness with real life buffalo grazing on wide, scattered, ranches. Then, like manna from heaven, I saw a large casino with a hotel attached. Yeah, buddy! I'm not into gambling, but I knew casinos often had inexpensive alcohol and food, to go along with a lot of lovely women. The room was nice, and well within my per diem budget. Once I got back from a day's work, I went down to the bar and was dismayed to find nearly the entire casino filled with blue-haired oldies, mostly gambling and smoking cigarettes. That scene repeated the next night. Damn.

During that period of my life, I was getting a lot of mail from Capital Law School, a small private institution in Columbus, Ohio, based on an inquiry that I frankly do not ever recall making. The school had a special place in my mind, because it was the first school to accept me as an applicant three years prior. Due to the cost and preference for a bigger school, I never really considered them as an option. I spurned them for the Buckeyes, but at some point, during the years after I left Ohio State's law school, I must have reached out to Capital to send me information about reapplying and starting over. Maybe I did it in a stupor, but I just do not remember when or how.

Anyway, I guess I considered this literature as some type of a "sign." And, I was growing tired of life on the road. I had a girlfriend at the time. I had met her at my local bar, and our relationship consisted of near constant drinking almost every night I was in town. I loved her, but I was feeling emotionally empty and lacking long-term focus.

I was dismayed that my boy Tommy was going to likely spend the rest of his life in prison. Reggie had fully developed a monster of a cocaine habit. Adrian turned to a life of crime toward the end of high school and was selling crack in urban Columbus. My "goody" friends, Chris and Claude, had careers in Cincinnati and Detroit, respectively, after they graduated with their college degrees in hand. I guess after spending several years sowing my oats and getting in some more of the partying I had missed out on while rushing through college, I was ready to plan on a career. I was tired of drinking so much. I was weary with being directionless. I applied to and was promptly accepted into Capital University Law School in the fall of 2000. I promised my family and myself, that I would this time finish what I started.

I set a good tone by starting out well at Capital. From the jump, I made a point to go to class and participate. There was a tiny number of black students in the school, and I made sure to be a part of the community by joining the Black Law Student Association (BLSA). I enjoyed the classes. I studied and participated. There were some classes I enjoyed more than others, favoring constitutional history and social justice related classes, more so than business related and contract law. I thrived in Torts (personal injury) achieving one of the highest grades in the class. I was still partying a lot and hard, with my on and off again girlfriend and various other

For Black Men/Ali Shakoor

friends. But I was consciously cutting back my intake, and I certainly concentrated on my school work. I showed up, stayed engaged and made good friends. I maintained over a 3-point grade average every semester I was in school.

One thing my partying ways caused me to miss out on was the knowledge and inclination to secure a proper summer internship. Frankly, I was just out of the loop as some of my classmates took the initiative to obtain high paying jobs as interns in law firms or state agencies. The summer after my first year in law school, for money, I went back to my old real estate research marketing gig on a contract basis. When my second year of law school started up, my first-year Property Law professor, a kind and brilliant but sickly older black man, recommended me for a teaching assistant position. The stipend from that job helped supplement my loans and partial scholarships for school and living expenses.

The reason why I am working in the criminal law field today, is because after my second year I was hired for a job as an intern at the Franklin County Prosecutor's Office through something for law students of color, called the "minority clerkship program." I worked there for several months, preparing files for discovery. I fell in love with the courtroom by watching many of the senior attorneys in live trials. I eventually switched over to working as an intern with the Franklin County Public Defender's Office, because they paid a little bit more. That's where I worked when I got my ill-fated DUI, and on through my graduation from law school.

Working at the PD's office in Columbus, Ohio allowed me direct contact with the accused. Part of my job included interviewing people prior to arraignment so that the lawyers knew what to discuss during bail hearings. I prepared minor motions pertaining to clients wanting to resolve warrants for missed court dates and other pretrial motions. Again, I was inspired by watching the attorneys at work during trial.

I finished strong during my final year at law school and graduated with honors, Cum Laude, with a 3.3 GPA. The foundation provided by my mother's insistence on raising us in suburban white schools meant that I was, unfortunately, the only black student in my class to graduate with honors. My partying at night and disengagement from many law school activities beyond BLSA, made me miss out on another crucial element of law school; perhaps the most important step, bar exam prep. I was embarrassingly clueless about preparing for the bar exam. I just knew I wanted to move somewhere warm. I was ignorant about the expensive and intensive process of preparing for the bar exam that most of my fellow students began during the second year. I did not take any of those evening bar prep classes like most students, and I did not even know where I wanted to take the bar exam. Luckily, I missed the deadline for the

Ohio bar exam and that ensured that I would accomplish my goal of leaving the state. When I was working on the road for the real estate gig, I fell in love with two parts of the country: first and foremost, the southwest (Southern California and Arizona) and secondly, Florida. A casual acquaintance informed me that she was preparing for the Florida bar exam and that there was still time to enroll.

Bet, I decided I was going to prepare to try and become a lawyer in Florida.

I simply did not have the money for an expensive bar prep course like BarBri, which is what most of my fellow students had already been long enrolled in. I searched online for a cheapo, bootleg, alternative and found something called MicroMash. None of my coworkers or small circle of law school friends had heard of it, but that was all I could afford. With some financial help from my mom, I paid the sign-up fees to take the Florida bar exam and purchased the MicroMash package, which consisted of books and computer disks. I was determined to pass on my first try, so I made one small, but very important decision to have my cable service removed from my apartment to reduce distractions. Thank goodness, being a basketball and football fanatic meant that I did not have to worry about missing any sports that I cared about during the middle of summer. The NBA Gods were also looking out for me and wanted me to pass the bar exam, because I cannot think of an NBA Finals in my lifetime that I gave less of a damn about than the San Antonio Spurs versus the New Jersey Nets.

I was disciplined and competitive. I greatly cut back on drinking and slutting around and fixed myself to a study schedule. My nature of enjoying solitude without feeling lonely really did me well during those long weeks. The bar exam was in Tampa, Florida and I was able to schedule an interview with the Hillsborough County Public Defender's Office while I was there. Later that summer while waiting for bar exam results, I also had an interview with a State Attorney's Office in Fort Lauderdale, Florida. Before I was properly awoken to the corruption of too many lying police officers, and the morally bankrupt War on Drugs, I actually used to want to be a prosecutor in order to eventually focus on violent crimes.

I felt very confident that I passed the exam, but one can never be certain about such things until the results come out. There are plenty of horror stories about people failing the bar exam multiple times. I have always been a pretty good test taker on things that I am naturally good at and interested in. My brain does not work well with math or anything resembling math, so that's one area where I have faltered. I've excelled at applying concepts to real life scenarios, involving people, places and circumstances. I could never be a doctor, scientist, engineer or an accountant. My brain does not work that way. I was born to be a lawyer, actor, teacher, writer, or activist. Similarly, you have a special set of skills or gifts, if you will. Foster that and make it work for you in a positive direction.

I have a good memory for things that interest me. I am not a genius and nor am I the hardest worker, but I work hard, and I am pretty smart. I needed a total combined score of 133 to pass the Florida bar exam. I easily passed with a 147. Not bad for a late start and studying alone with something called MicroMash. I notified the offices I interviewed with that I had passed the exam. I was offered a job as an attorney with the Hillsborough County Public Defender's Office in Tampa, Florida. My mom and I packed up my car and loaded a rented van just shy of Thanksgiving in 2003, then I embarked on the next chapters of my life in Florida. No matter what struggles I would encounter as a black man in this country, particularly in the South, I was fortified with an advanced degree to be able to earn an honest living. Ali A. Shakoor, J.D.

My years as a public defender were tough, as I dealt with health problems. It took a while for my asthma to adapt to the Tampa, Florida climate while I struggled to find the right medicine. On top of that, I developed a hiatal hernia which caused me constant painful heartburn. The office I worked for was a miserable experience; political, overworked and underpaid. I started out as a rising star, but my health problems and a souring attitude led me to feeling isolated and angry. Without my girlfriend Tanya at the time, I am not sure I would have made it. We did have fun on most weekends and the occasional vacation. But working as a public defender in Tampa during those days, was the most miserable three years of my working life. Nearly every morning on my way to work, I would start the day with my theme song: Goodie Mobb and Outkast's *Git Up, Git Out*.

Yet still, I gained expertise learning some very important skills for legal practice and the confidence to handle complex trials. It was a good training ground. Importantly, crucially, I learned how the game is rigged against people of color and poor people in general. One example where I learned that I am not one for "going along to get along" in the legal community, involved a raging asshole of an assistant state attorney--a Hispanic white lady, who I'll call "Melissa"--and a client of mine she tried to railroad to pad her stats. This is another important lesson in my early legal life, where I knew I possessed moral courage and that I was an advocate as opposed to a fucking *esquire*. One thing I will never accept that comes along with the legal profession, is the elitism. It is infuriating to me and conflicts with my core values.

So, I had this client, an uneducated middle-aged white guy who worked to get by; handyman type stuff, maybe some construction. He was charged with possession of crack cocaine, but it was a bogus charge and a completely unwinnable case for the state. He was in the backseat of a car occupied by a total of three people. Not that it matters for legal purposes, but the car did not belong to my client. After an apparently legal traffic stop, the driver allegedly gave permission for the police to search the car. The piece of crack rock was found under the driver's seat, in front of my client. All the occupants of the car denied knowledge of rock. The driver and my client were arrested, because the rock was closest to them.

This was a case of alleged "constructive possession," meaning the rock was not in actual possession (on the person, with nobody else having equal access). However, for the state to prevail on a constructive possession charge, the state of Florida must prove that multiple people have *knowledge and access* to the contraband. In the case I am talking about, nobody admitted to knowing anything about the dope. Without a confession, the prosecution had no case.

After meeting my client at arraignment, we scheduled an appointment for him to come to my office to discuss the facts of his case. To qualify for a public defender, my client was indigent, meaning he was low on the socioeconomic scale, unable to afford his own attorney. Visiting me at the office and coming to court for hearings meant that my client had to miss work at his low paying gigs. I filed the appropriate motion to dismiss, filled with the proper caselaw. The gist of the motion was that if everything provided by the prosecution in discovery was true, they still could not win the case at trial. Now what a lot of prosecutors would do in a situation like this is "stand silent" on the motion, thereby signaling to the judge that it's okay to dismiss the case. Some prosecutors start out by playing it like Melissa did, and file a response challenging the motion as if there are facts in dispute.

To the detriment of the defendants, what happens next is a game of "chicken," as the prosecutor fakes like they have a winning case in hopes that the defendant caves all scared and takes some type of bullshit probation offer. More shamefully, prosecutors try to wear down the defendants by having them to go to court so often, missing work and other responsibilities. The prosecutor just wants a conviction, a stat to add to their resume, in hopes of advancement up the office chain in a thirst for more money and power. Also, some prosecutors are just sadists. Hopefully, the client trusts his lawyer that the prosecutor will eventually drop the charges based on the law.

The situation with Melissa and I really went sideways after my client had already come to court for the third or fourth time. On one particular day, my client and I were ready for "trial" i.e. the state announcing that they were dropping the case. Instead, Melissa stated that she was asking for a continuance based on some crap about needing to speak to more witnesses. More witnesses for a fucking crack rock case? A continuance? My indigent client would be missing work for more court dates, so Melissa could hold out for a case she couldn't win. Bullshit. I kept my cool and calmly stated my objection to the continuance, due to the state not having a valid basis and the hardship to my client. Melissa then rolled her eyes and dismissed me on the record by stating she was not even going to "dignify" my objection. I kept my cool, but, *I'm-not-the-one*. I did not know who the hell she thought she was, being so blatantly disrespectful on the record. Was she just being an asshole? Was it a racial thing? I had no answers, but it was extremely dismissive and unprofessional in a courtroom full of people. The judge granted the state's continuance, because that is typically what criminal judges do whenever the prosecution allegedly needs more time. This entire situation was inconsiderate to my hardworking client.

Moments later, when I approached the prosecutor's table to get an offer for another client from one of her colleagues, Melissa asked why I had such an obsession with this "filthy low life" of a defendant. I calmly remarked on her elitist snobbery and kept it moving. A few days before my client's next "trial" date, I was in court on a Thursday afternoon, and it was a typically slow end of the week session. There was only one prosecutor in the courtroom, along with me, two other public defenders, and the judge with his staff. I was determined to set some matters straight after the previous experience with Melissa. For what it's worth, my fellow public defenders were also black that day, and the prosecutor was a Latina whom I had always had a cordial working relationship with. Towards the end of our court session, I told the prosecutor that I wanted her to call Melissa to the courtroom to address the case involving the bogus crack rock charge. She called down to her office, but Melissa had taken the day off. Oh well, I tried.

I made sure everything was on the record as I called the case last. I explained to the judge the nature of my previous motion to dismiss and how I was on sound legal ground. I also alluded to the peculiar handling of the particular case considering the multiple hearings, latest continuance and extreme hardship on my client's ability to maintain employment. Moreover, Melissa had not provided any more discovery evidence relating to my client's case, so therefore, case law warranted a dismissal of the charges. If Melissa intended to put forth evidence at the "trial" that was not previously provided to me, as required by law, I was going to move for an appropriate motion on the matter and request sanctions. The judge just stared at me bemused like he knew exactly what I was getting at and took the issue under advisement. At that point, I just *dropped the mic* and started packing up my stuff. My two colleagues, both more experienced than I, just stared at me warily like I was planning a slave rebellion which they wanted no part in.

The next morning at work my direct supervisor "Donald," called me into his office. Donald asked me what happen in court the previous day regarding my case and Melissa, since he was not there. I calmly explained the whole situation. He did not seem too concerned but said that Melissa wanted to meet in the judge's chambers to discuss what I put on the record and wanted her supervisor with her. So, Donald was supposed to accompany me to the meeting. I thought, okay, whatever, she sure as hell better not ask for another continuance, though.

Donald and I walked over to the judge's chambers and Melissa was already there with her boss. Since Melissa requested the meeting, the ball was in her court to get on with her issues. She basically spent several minutes explaining how ethical she was and how she valued her reputation, and *blah freaking blah freaking blah*. She did not request another continuance. When it was my turn, I really had nothing to say. I just shrugged that I stood by what I already stated and that my client was ready for "trial." The judge just seemed tickled by this little soap opera but declined to get in the weeds on the topic. He changed the subject to some other general scheduling matters, kept things light, and we were probably out of there in about five minutes.

My annoyance did not rise until the way back to our office, as Donald gave me a mini lecture about how we need to have a civil relationship with opposing counsel and not let personal matters interfere. Fine enough. I was certainly not the one that escalated anything until she tried to treat me like something unworthy on the record, in open court, and most importantly, was playing games with my client's livelihood. She was driven by a desire to bully my client into padding her conviction stats and a bizarre personal vendetta.

Look, I have never bought into the whole elitist *"esquire"* bullshit. Melissa and I were lawyers, with a particular set of skills and talents. My client had other gifts. Nobody is better than the other. Just as my client came to my office with a problem, I would have to go to him, clueless, if I had a car issue that needed to be handled or construction done. We all have roles in this country, and nobody has a right to look down upon another. Melissa showed her character when she dismissed my client as being a so-called "dirty low life" and questioned the reason for my advocacy. Melissa came from Tampa money. I came from a socioeconomic background similar to my indigent client. If I ever got into legal problems for some of the wayward shit I did in my youth, my mother would have had to request the services of the public defender. More than that, I knew people like my client, or at least new their kids. I had lived around them and partied with some of them. These are people, flawed, just like all of us, trying to get by. Where people like my client encounter situations where one could be found in a car with a crack rock, people of Melissa's ilk had their powder cocaine at posh parties and country club bathrooms. The double standard is infuriating.

Anyway, the next "trial" day my client held firm rejecting all offers; even time-served and court costs. We sat and waited for the courtroom assignment and jury selection time. Do you know that petty Melissa waited until the very last goddamn case, and then announced she was dropping all charges against my client? She did not have the decency to accept her losing hand and allow my client to get back to his job sooner. My client and I shook hands, then he went back to his life of hard labor. Melissa came from money, married into money, was working a job she would soon leave to carry on life as a "Real Privileged Housewife of South Tampa," and provided a story I will never forget. I am proud to be nothing like her, nor what she represents.

The point of the story is that taking advantage of educational or career opportunities does not mean that you cannot stay true to yourself. As I stand in courtrooms, I take with me all my life experiences. I maintain my sense of racial pride and awareness. I will not get played for a fool or taken advantage of, at least not without an appropriate response. Just keep everything in the proper context. My sister's case was devastating and emotional, and I certainly had some *"When keeping it real goes wrong"* moments, but I am stronger for it. My convictions and code will always fuel me to fight for justice. I have an aversion to pretension and corruption.

I was fortunate enough to escape the PD's office in December of 2006, in route to the best job I have ever had working for a state agency as a postconviction attorney for death row inmates. This office environment is supportive. We do very important work. The job fits my fighting for the underdog nature, and it incorporates my love for sociology, psychology, U.S. history and the law. I have met some good people in my life at work. For most of my time at this gig, I have been the only black attorney in the whole office. These colleagues of mine have been there for me through health problems and my family's problem. My conservative supervisors particularly had my back; offering trust, patience and letters of support, when I was dealing with the Florida Bar. My bosses and colleagues trust my judgment and value my legal acumen.

This job has allowed me to make a good living and rise into a supervisory position. I am doing very important work that I am passionate about. The first time I argued a case in front of the Florida Supreme Court, I really soaked it all in; I was fascinated and bemused about how the various turns in my life took me to that point. Now, after six arguments before the highest court in the state, along with complex filings circulating through various stages of the judiciary, all the way up to the United States Supreme Court, and a recent oral argument before the United States Court of Appeals for the Eleventh Circuit, I am satisfied that I have earned what I have accomplished and that I certainly belong.

I even parlayed my career experiences into a side gig teaching at the University of Phoenix. It started several years ago as I went looking for a way to supplement my income and take advantage of some extra free time in my private life. I have taught courses on criminal justice and the U.S. Constitution. It has been rewarding and I can certainly see myself teaching into my elder years at a major university. Professor Ali A. Shakoor, J.D.? I never would have seen this coming twenty-five years ago.

Getting the J.D. also allowed me to make a difference in ways that I did not fully understand as an overwhelmed and miserable public defender. When I first entered the felony division, I was handling some low-level crack possession cases. At one point when interviewing clients in jail, I had this old Haitian brother named "Moses." He was only in his late fifties, but he looked much older. He was basically homeless, and his record consisted of trespass and drug related charges. As I was discussing his case with him, he seemed dead to rights on a crack cocaine possession charge. I did not seem to have a viable motion to suppress. I told Moses that the prosecutors were offering a year and a day in prison, or we could take the case to trial and risk five years. Our discussion grew temperamental on both sides, but I am sure I was at fault for feeling frustrated. I was lecturing him about life choices, and he was schooling me about being a better lawyer and getting his case reduced to a misdemeanor paraphernalia possession. I may have visited him once more and had a similar discussion, then by the time pretrial rolled around my trip to Moses University proved helpful, as the prosecutor did indeed reduce his case to a misdemeanor charge and time-served. Moses winked at me and took the plea as I smiled back at him.

Over the years, going on sixteen years now, I have seen Moses well over a dozen times in different areas of Tampa, mostly in Ybor City, an entertainment district where he would hold court by singing or generally walking the street. As the years have gone by, I've seen Moses gain weight and seemingly get younger. He has seen me walking with different women, in different states of sobriety, but he always seems to see me first, as he calls out, "Hey, Mr. Shakoor!" I smile, turn around, exchange some dap, and always give him a twenty. We always have the same conversation the past several times, and more recently when I was walking in Ybor City with my sister, niece and nephew one early evening while they were visiting me for spring break. I am proud they got a chance to meet him, as Mr. Moses went through his routine of showing off his most recent chip indicating many years of sobriety, and he said that I was instrumental in helping him straighten his life out. He can recall detail discussions that I just barely remember. Mr. Moses talks about how much he appreciates how I spoke to him and how I must have saw something redeemable and unpolished in him.

My law degree has been instrumental in helping me personally, and I have made a difference in positively resolving some very major cases. But on the micro level, it does my heart really well to know that Mr. Moses believes I affected his life in a positive way. Education and skills are not just about working hard and keeping out of trouble. It is not all just geared toward making money. It is also about the people we connect with, and our shine rubbing off on and filling people who need it more than we can ever know.

This long chapter, in which I shared a great deal of deeply personal information about my life experiences, serves as a crucial reminder that a strong educational foundation can allow you to recover from all types of mistakes and failures. Particularly during this white supremacist resurgence, and Trumpism, that follows as a backlash to the Obama era. Please build on all the skills that you possess. We have all had struggles in life, be it struggles with depression, romance, substance abuse, or just the drama that is always waiting around some corner. You need something to fall back on that allows you to strive in a positive light. You must pay your bills. You should support your family. For me, it was the law, for you it may be any other field or skillset. Just foster your gifts in a legal and positive way. This is really the best way to stay out of the criminal justice system. It also brings pride and meaning to your life.

Chapter Eight

Seeking Positive Relationships

Reggie and Tommy were like family to me but distancing myself from them to a certain degree and concentrating on my education was a game-changing decision towards success. In the previous chapter, I mentioned how both were there for me at a crucial point in my life as I was experimenting and stepping out of my square. They were there for all my firsts. We also always had each other's backs. I would offer a ride or lend my truck if a brother needed a ride to work and they would do the same.

Tommy particularly helped me out of a couple embarrassing situations. One time, he apparently saved my life. We were good and high, walking around some festival in downtown Columbus. I cannot recall if it was Ribfest or JazzFest, but it was some type of "Get out with your homies to holla at some fine sistas Fest." As we were walking, I stopped to point and laugh at this dude who I truly believed was wearing a big goofy looking mask. Tommy, harshly and in a panic, told me to shut the fuck up and quickly defused the situation. That was my first encounter with a local Columbus, Ohio legend that was known as "Big Head Tony." I didn't know anything about Hydrocephalus! Big Head Tony was a local alleged drug dealer and general baller, who had this serious disease. According to the story going around, he also had a lot of money due to donating his body to "science," for medical study after he died. Tommy and the crew had my clueless back, in this instance, and many others.

When I was first trying to figure out *how* to drink, I had some shameful moments. I recall one time we were hanging out at Tommy's older cousin's crib, a dude by the name of Jackson. Jackson also grew up in Worthington. He was a few years older, handsome, and a talented former high school football player. Jackson was having a party on one particular night. Thinking back on what I indulged in on the evening, I get queasy and embarrassed. See, back then, for whatever reason, despite better options available, my boys and I drank either malt liquor or cheap-ass wine. Our malt liquor, a heinous beer-like substance that could be used to clean a butcher room floor, was usually either Old English (O.E.) or St. Ides. For "wine" we would drink either Mad Dog 20/20 or Cisco. The girls circulating in and out of the crew typically stuck with Boone's Farm. A quick Internet search on these titles from my youth has taught me that these alcoholic beverages are made cheaply, priced cheaply, high in alcohol content, and geared towards the poor and homeless. Yeah.

Anyway, on the night of the party, I decided to enjoy a 40 oz bottle of O.E. Then I got hungry, as we made a run to McDonald's. Obviously, the quarter pounder meal soaked up all my buzz, so I bought a bottle of Cisco to extend a party that was just expiring, regardless of my ambitions. I recall sitting on the stairsteps and watching television, while getting that familiar watery taste in my mouth and feeling dizzy. The next moment I remember is sitting in the passenger side of my own pickup truck as Tommy was driving me home to my mom's house. He explained that I had painted his cousin's bathroom with foul vomit, and he had cleaned it up for me. We got kicked out and he was driving me home. He explained this to me in a calm fashion, without anger or judgment. It was just a fact of life. His homeboy had a bad night, and he had to handle it. I think of that whenever I take Tommy's calls from prison in Ohio, and when I send him something every year on his birthday. I am glad I was not with him the night of the shooting, but he will always be family.

It is crucially important to separate love from obligation. Reggie and Tommy always pushed me toward my strength in academics. I remember having a drug fueled evening with Reggie at some party in the late '90s, when during a moment of realness through our haze of weed and coke, Reggie asked, "When you going back to law school, dawg?" I thought of that moment sitting in the lounge, right before I walked into the courtroom for the 11th Circuit Court of Appeals, in Atlanta, Georgia. At that appellate circuit stage, I was just one level below the United States Supreme Court. I'm glad I went back to law school, dawg.

I am currently as happy, successful, and as comfortable in my skin as I have ever been. A couple years ago, I got a call from Reggie while I was on vacation with my girlfriend on South Beach in Miami. I paid cash for the Easter Weekend vacation, and we drove down in my lady's Mercedes convertible. I was lying in bed preparing for an evening out, when Reggie called me fresh out of rehab, just checking in as we had not spoken in well over a year. Reggie was in between jobs and figuring out where he was going to be living in our Ohio hometown, hoping it would be with his on and off again ex-girlfriend. The dichotomy of this development and our respective lifestyles at the time, altered my mood for the rest of the evening in a whimsical fashion. He was family, a former mentor, and was trying to pull his life together while on the verge of homelessness.

I spoke with Reggie one time after that. I was home in Ohio for my typical summer vacation trip in early June. We were texting and playing phone tag, trying to figure out a time to hook up, but our schedules did not allow it to happen, unfortunately. We eventually chatted the evening before I was going to fly back to Tampa. He was in a much better frame of mind and was back to work at a landscaping gig where he was a manager. The company kept bringing him back no matter how many times he relapsed, because of his work ethic and he was so good at bringing in business. He was also living with his lady, just as he had wanted. My man sounded good; healthy and goal oriented. He was on the born-again Christian tip and focusing on sobriety. We verbally dapped up and committed to getting together when I would be back in town for the holidays.

A few months later, in the first week of October in2017, I received a text one morning while getting ready for work. It was the moment I had previously feared would come one day. Chris told me that he got word from a trusted source that Reggie had passed away in his sleep early that morning. I drove to work through teary eyes and received confirmation from his family online. Unfortunately, blood clots took my friend out. Reggie called his mother, a nurse, on the night he died while complaining about leg cramps and problems breathing. Reggie's mom told him to call an ambulance or head to the hospital immediately. Reggie never made it, dying in his sleep. The autopsy results indicated that he had gotten clean from drugs.

The shit really broke my heart. A death has not hit me this hard, and personally, since my granddad passed almost thirty years ago. I always hoped Reggie and I would someday be old men laughing about old times on a porch somewhere. Reggie left a sixteen-year-old son, who he adored. The boy looks just like him. He is at the age that Reggie and I were when we first became homies. At this point, all I can do is be an uncle to Reggie's son, and "*Sing About…*" Reggie, in the way that Kendrick Lamar wrote about. I know Reggie was proud of me and wanted the best for me through my elder years. I do not have survivor's remorse, as I am secure in knowing that I am a product of my choices and a lot of good luck. That said, out of our little clique, Tommy is still in the Ohio state penal system and Reggie has passed on after seemingly beating a brutal long-term drug addiction. I take the best of what we had, cherish it, and pass the knowledge along. I also have a duty to tell the truth and serve out the cautionary tales for ya'll brothers out there.

I am sure you have people in your crew who want the best for you, to take advantage of any way out of the pipeline. If on the other hand, you have people in your life who are all about negativity and nihilism, you must let them go. No matter what they have done for you or how much you consider them to be family, you should love yourself more than you love them. Another person giving up on any sense of freedom and happiness should not create a barrier to your goals toward happiness.

I still have old friends that I've remained close with. We live in different states, so we may only see each other a couple different times a year, if that. We are relatively successful. Our lives do not involve criminality or any other type of perpetual negative drama. Fortunately, we have not fallen victim to the vices of substance abuse addiction. We are not saints and without snitching, I can appreciate that we have had our share of glorious fun over the years, but it is positive. It's about shared interests in Ohio State football and other sports, private jokes and memories of growing up in the '70s, '80s and '90s. It is about hip hop, stand-up comics, TV and movies, as we have jokes and opinions about pop culture. It is being there for each other and appreciating the power of friendship in the same ways that Preach and Cochise did.

You must also set boundaries and make decisions about actual family, regardless of blood relations. In all forms of animal species, the initial family unit is the key to positive emotional development. We require some form of loving affection from the moment we enter this world. It is essential for our survival. I discussed in a previous chapter why it is important to be a good parent. Unfortunately, not every black man learned lessons during an encouraging upbringing. I recently attended a conference where one of the presenters showed a video clip called The Still-Face Experiment, created by Dr. Edward Tronick. The short clip shows the effect of a parent's expression and temperament on the early psyche of a baby. From our earliest stages of development, the stressors that rub off from adults have a direct impact on us. But it does not even have to be a parent. We all come from a similar traumatic entry into this world, and the first encounters we experience shape our psychological development. And the people we grew up around the most, form a bond to us based on familiarity if nothing else. However, you cannot let the reality of "family" override the need to ultimately do what is in your best interests going forward; meaning the health and well-being of yourself and any children you may be responsible for. We all have a relative or more who is toxic.

Over the years, I have done a Google search on my evil stepfather every now and then to see what is going on in his life and maybe decide to work up the desire to seek him out and confront him. Maybe I would send him some details on my sister's case to show him the hell he created; the cyclical perversion unwittingly sought out by women who survived abuse. The man has never maintained an online presence. No Myspace, no Facebook, no LinkedIn, and no Twitter. I wanted vengeance, but I did not want to ruin my life with legal problems or becoming involved with the criminal justice system. I wanted to believe that he was suffering, and I wanted him to apologize to my mom and sister. I would Google him a few times throughout the year, but nothing came up. I could have hired an investigator or paid into one of those online person search sites, but that was more energy than I was willing to commit regarding that man. I was never sure how I wanted to deal with that unresolved issue which was the root of so many problems in my life.

The fear. The anger. The guilt. Ultimately, I got a small bit of redemption through fighting injustice in Franklin County, Ohio. The man was only in my life for about fourteen years, but his wicked presence affected me for years afterward. If my mother had not divorced him when she did, I would have eventually become a serious criminal or a drug addict, and my sister, maybe a worse life. Choices have consequences, and my mother trying to make things work with such a horrid, ultimately irredeemable man, almost destroyed herself and her children. I am grateful that she finally found the strength to leave and become the best mother a person could hope for, and more than making up for past errors in judgment.

One summer day my online searches lead me to a few different sites, and the last one hosted an obituary confirming his death. Azeem Bilaal Shakoor died on December 26, 2016 at the age of sixty-two years old. He was living in Silver Spring, Maryland. It was maddening to read some of the laudatory details about his life, but alas, that is the nature of obituaries. Looking at his face became a temporary habit on that day, a face aged and fuller, but with the same penetrating eyes; eyes lying to those who didn't know his secret life of unfathomable misogyny and cruelty. Perhaps he changed as he succumbed to what's described in the obituary as some unnamed disease that forced an "early retirement," and then later lead to his premature death. Maybe those people in his life during the final years knew a changed man. I doubt it, but I do not know. I do know that not one word was mentioned in the obituary about his sole child, my sister. He and his family can try to erase the past, but the past always lingers for my family. The key is how you deal with it. My mother, sister, and I are stronger people now, survivors. A decade or so ago, I would have taken some time after reading about the death to get into my feelings through music and intoxicants, in celebration and cursing the man good riddance. Instead, after emailing the online links to my mom and sister, I had a productive day at work, came home and had a great gym workout punctuated by a long hard run, and then got back to these here pages.

Enough about that dead man. The point I want to convey is that you <u>must</u> eliminate abusive people from your life and the lives of those close to you—as much as you can control such matters—as soon as possible. It is essential for a happy, healthy, hopeful, and productive existence.

Your family may be involved with criminal behavior, not because they are bad people, but they need a means to survive. But a lifetime of criminal behavior always leads to death or imprisonment. You are reading this book because you want to avoid such a fate. At this point in your life, you must be able to cut the cord without fear and unburdened by feelings of loyalty. You can do so without judgment, as institutional racism has limited many opportunities for our people. Perhaps those you are leaving behind eventually will find a way to live a straight crime-free life. You know how difficult that can be in some communities. You must look out for yourself. If they love you, if they care about your future and sense of personal responsibility, your family will support your decision to leave a life of crime.

You can also create a "family" with people who provide a legitimate and positive support system. It is not always about blood.

For Black Men/Ali Shakoor

One of my favorite movies is *Boogie Nights*. It is set in the world of the 1970s porn industry in Los Angeles, but the themes are universal: rejected, alienated, lonely, confused, and broken-spirited people looking for someone to understand and love them. This is a wild and sweet movie, but in your more normal world there is a mentor that is looking out for your best interests. You have or will discover a set of friends that want nothing but the best for you and vice versa. You will have a love interest in your life, who you will want to build a future with and provide for a family. Remember the first love you spent hours talking on the phone with from the time you laid down at night to chat before bed, until the sun rose with your voice hoarse and dry, as you were finally ready to say goodbye until next time? That feeling can be combined with reaching the point in life where you are ready to commit to someone who wants to love, help, fight for, and grow old with you. Are you ready for love?

Romance is another area where it is important to stay out of negative situations. For all the rhetoric out there about avoiding "drama" how often over the years have we all been involved with the wrong person? Regardless of whether you are gay, bisexual. straight, or unsure, I am talking to all my brothers right now. Find a mate who will bring out the best in you and provide joy into your life. So many brothas get caught up in emotionally unhealthy situations. That often leads to violence. I have discussed how it is unacceptable to use violence to deal with your anger; particularly when it comes to your interactions with women. You must stay away from relationships that involve abusive conflict, which you remain in because the sex is crazy good, or the good times are so temporarily fulfilling.

It is human to disagree. Occasionally disagreements lead to necessary arguments. But it cannot be chronic, with over the top hurtful name-calling. It is bad for the psyche. You need someone in your life as a steady romantic partner, only if it is mutually about building up each other's confidence to reach maximum potential. You can spot the ones trying to crack at your self-esteem early, if you are paying attention. The little things like criticizing your interests and questioning your ability to better yourself, is a sign to exit the relationship at the early stages. Such folks are trying to create a codependent relationship based on mutual sabotage. Stay away from that shit. If you recognize some of those negative qualities in yourself, own it, stop it, and if necessary, seek counseling to put an end to it. You cannot improve yourself and live a crime-free life if you have a compulsion to tear people down. In the end, you are destroying yourself.

Also, you know if you are the controlling, creeper, stalker, type, just as you can recognize to avoid it in others. Some clichés are fundamentally true. It is a fact that "hurt people, hurt people." We as men, in particular, have exhibited an obscene desire to control women. It is part of the DNA of American society. It is more deeply rooted than institutional racism. We know this nation was founded by racist and misogynistic white men, otherwise known as the "founding fathers." But also understand that black men were granted the right to vote, via the Fifteenth Amendment in 1870, over fifty years before women were given the right based on the Nineteenth Amendment in 1920. Look what this country did to Hillary Clinton. We have never had a female president in this country's history, and despite Mrs. Clinton's faults, for her to lose an election to this deranged "President Grab Em by the Pussy," is an indictment on this patriarchal nation.

This country is as bad as any in western civilization, once you examine problems that still exist today like unequal pay for the same work, slut-shaming hypocrisy, infringements on reproductive choices, and domestic violence. A man can enjoy time with a woman on any evening and make a choice about whether to have sex, and with the option of changing our minds at *any* point in the evening. A woman encounters the legitimate risk of being raped any time she is alone with a man, and then subsequently questioned about whether she brought the act on herself by allegedly "asking for it." Men must understand propaganda and theories that contribute to this disgrace of designating women as inferior beings. It starts with major religions.

Look my brothers, follow whatever religious paths you need to stay out of prison, or none at all. If you choose a religious faith, as all permit you to decide which tenets of a holy book you are supposed to follow in the manner of a buffet, choose against oppression. Understand that countless evil white folks in this country spent centuries finding justifications for slavery, Jim Crow, and the horror that came with it, in the New Testament of the Christian Bible. I am not picking on Christianity, so to speak, but I will address a few issues since it is the dominant religion in this country. You must understand how Christianity is used to suppress women.

The mind games start with the very basic principle of referring to God in the masculine sense, as in "Our Father," "Heavenly Father," "The man upstairs." You get the point. We have taken this for granted all our lives, but it absolutely deserves scrutiny as the Christian Bible, which was written by men, is mandating that some invisible, intangible, alleged presence, is a masculine figure. Consider how Christians depict the origin of humans. The first alleged human being on this earth is called Adam, a man. The woman, Eve, comes into being by God, from a piece of Adam's rib. These first two alleged humans are supposed to be happy and perfect until original sin becomes the fault of Eve, for being tempted by a talking snake in the Garden of Eden. Eve is supposedly the cause of all human sin???Let us just stop right there, so you can see that

Christians are rigging it against women from the jump. Islam can be another tool of oppression when it comes to women being controlled and dominated by men, but this obvious point can be explored on your own. Just recognize what and how you worship. Focus it in a way that is about love, freedom, and equality.

Believe what you want, dabble in what you will, but do not traffic in the oppression of women. Interpret your holy books in a way that disavows bigotry and oppression. Men, like all humans, can be insecure. Some men deal with that insecurity by trying to control women. We as men are generally stronger and bigger, so some men often try to dominate women with physicality. The inability to deal with some of your own personal issues may cause you to forcefully dominate another person, and usually women (and children) bear the brunt of it.

Sexual activity is the driving force of our existence. It is how we procreate and remain. And when it comes to the feeling, as Jamie Foxx said as the titular character in the movie biopic, *Ray*, "Ain't nothing better than sex." We as men understand what we love about it and why we need it. Think about it from a woman's perspective. Women can generally have it whenever they want it. We as men pursue it, and sometimes obsess over it. The quality of the magical consummated event itself, requires the male participant to not only maintain an erection, but to last, and to know how to stroke. This is a source of anxiety and again, insecurity, for some men. It sometimes causes such men to lash out, joined with some preexisting sadistic tendencies to control and dominate. Controlling women on a global level politically and fueled with religious theories of alleged superiority, is all mixed up in these issues. The burden of being a good lover, instead of being bemused and patient about it, causes some men to combine that insecurity, fear, and anger, with other issues that boil up and create perpetrators. Recognize the rigged game that women live through in this land of white patriarchy. Understand that emotional and physical violence is completely intolerable.

Life is all about a series of relationships, from womb to casket. It is essential to focus on putting yourself in circumstances that are about nothing but love, fun, respect, empathy and all that is positive. Surround yourself with good people and put yourself in the right kinds of situations that set you on the path toward a healthy life.

Chapter Nine

Understanding the Law

Use the law of the land to your advantage. We are a nation of laws. And as horrifically as our people in this country have been abused and deprived of justice over the years, it is still the law; particularly the United States Constitution, which has served as the tool to lift us up. Mastery of the law can lead you to freedom. With every advancement that our people have made in this country, from the moment we were brought here after the unconscionable cruelty of the Middle Passage, to the present moment, the salvation has been the United States Constitution. The irony is interesting, though. The "founding fathers" were uniformly racist to varying degrees. Some of that goes to the deplorable tenor of the times, but it is simply a reality that there was a desire of white men to own and control people at the inception of our nation. Racism and patriarchy are part of America's DNA. I cannot even bear to devote time to the Native Americans who were here before the Europeans and had their property and humanity wiped away as America was created. It was evil. Please take in those stories during your own time of study, as I can only focus on trying to help my black brothers in the confines of these pages.

Much of the Constitution was not meant to apply to the rights of black people, or women either for that matter. Our people were considered property. It is bitter to consider that the white men who stole this country insisted upon a belief in independence and freedom to apply only to themselves and maintained the entitlement to own other human beings. Granted, some of those white men advocated against the continuation of slavery as the Constitution was being adopted, but as usual, not enough white people cared enough to fight for our freedom. Sure, a Civil War may have been sooner, rather than later, but they were fighting for the freedom and civil rights of all humans in this new land or they were not.

The Constitution mandated that representation in the House of Representatives was based on a state's population, as well as the determination of taxes levied. There was contentious debate about how to account for the fact that the vast majority of slaves were in the South. Therefore, came the derogatory 3/5 Clause, which determined that the slave population in the South would account for 3/5 of the free population, specifically:

Article 1, Section 2, Paragraph 3 of the U.S. Constitution, says:

> Representatives and direct Taxes shall
> be apportioned among the several
> States which may be included within
> this Union, according to their
> respective Numbers, which shall be
> determined by adding to the whole

For Black Men/Ali Shakoor

> Number of free Persons, including
> those bound to Service for a Term of
> Years, and excluding Indians not
> taxed, <u>three fifths of all other Persons.</u>

The white men who wrote the Constitution also made a point to protect the importation of our people like chattel for another twenty years, in order to appease the slaveholding states. The motherfuckers even saw fit to include a clause to protect the return of slaves trying to escape to freedom. The Fugitive Slave Clause reads:

> No person held to service or labour in one state, under the laws thereof, escaping into another, shall, in consequence of any law or regulation therein, be discharged from such service or labour, but shall be delivered up on claim of the party to whom such service or labour may be due.

As you looked over the previous two clauses I cited, you probably notice something interesting as it relates to what I have been discussing. There is no direct mention of race or "slaves." The "founding fathers" understood the concept of perception, if not shame. They knew the monumental task they were undertaking. While being influenced by texts as old as the Magna Carta, those white men understood the Constitution would be studied and analyzed as long as life exists on this planet. Coded language was a tool of the whites from the outset. However, we have been able to use the white man's perception concerns, and often, true belief in doing the right thing, to our advantage as Americans. From the amendments that followed the end of the Civil War, on through the attempted dismantling of some progress today, it is the rule of law that cannot only keep us from going to prison but may even provide a tunnel beyond the prison walls to freedom.

Yes, the Constitution can be a tool to legally escape from prison. Through strength of character and intelligence, and the luck of having the right judge, many former prisoners have successfully fought to litigate their way out of state and federal prison. They have used the law to fight issues such as wrongful convictions negated by evidence of actual innocence. Others have gotten illegal sentences reduced.

Learn and understand the laws of the jurisdictions in which you live.

As I discuss some legal issues in this chapter, understand that I am only licensed to practice in Florida. I have never planned on taking another bar exam or making a request to join a bar in another state ever again. I doubt I will change my mind. Moreover, in resolving my issue with the Florida Bar, I hammered down negotiations to end my case by telling the bar prosecutor, "Put in there that I'll never join a case in another state pro hac vice ever again," so I could get the skeptical white judge to finally accept my plea agreement, as he rejected the initial settlement that I had negotiated with the bar prosecutor. It worked, and I will get to that a little more in a minute, but understand, what I am discussing in this chapter is not legal advice. I can only tell you about the law in general fashion and based on my own experiences with Florida law. This "disclaimer" is not unique to me, as lawyers in general hope to keep state bars out of their pockets and not give them a way of misconstruing basic legal discussion, which can be "prosecuted" as "unlicensed practice of law." Anyway, with that stuff out of the way let us get back to using the law to stay out of the joint.

We are going to work backwards in the criminal justice process a little bit, since we have already discussed how knowledge of the law can get you out of prison. The judge is the final step between freedom and incarceration. They have all the power--within the confines of the Constitution and state law--but enough power to destroy your life and leave your family devastated. When I was battling the Florida Bar, by myself, without a lawyer, I had one agenda: (1). I would not apologize. (2). I would not rehabilitate the abhorrent conduct of the people in Franklin County, Ohio. (3). I would not throw my family under the bus and (4). I would not be suspended, let alone disbarred.

With those caveats, I was willing to accept my sanctions for losing my cool and going rogue in a desperate attempt to protect my niece from sexual abuse. The Constitution is inapplicable to bar prosecutions, as no liberty interest is at stake. Like any profession, practicing law is called a "privilege." I did not have the right to call witnesses to testify, if they did not want to. Meaning, I could not put my sister's Franklin County judge on the stand, or the guardian ad litem, or the opposing counsel, or my sister's ex-husband.

Importantly, I did not have a right to a jury. So, with all of that and the cost of the "prosecution" mounting against me in real dollars, I certainly did not trust the judge--a white man who was already being blatantly biased on the record, to the extent that I stood up in court and asked if he was engaging in ex parte conversations with witnesses from Ohio--, would not protect fellow white legal professionals and "the system." In short, I resolved my case, even though I was not at all happy about how things played out, and the false things alleged against my family and me. I settled, because things only would have gotten more expensive and worse for me, in what I perceived as a rigged system against people in my predicament. I settled because my family was under a lot of stress, and there were other ways to protect my niece and to absolutely expose the injustice. I am comfortable with my decision, all things considered.

You can only imagine the type of sympathy and empathy I have for people facing the dilemma of pleading to something they did not do, or less than they are culpable of, just to avoid a prison sentence. There is no doubt in my mind that I had clients plead to things they were innocent of, and only to avoid the risk of going to trial. It is heartbreaking to see such an internal wager played out. Often, the mother or father is afraid of leaving their children stuck in the foster care system, if they had the horrid misfortune of being sent to prison for a long stretch.

As a public defender, there were two judges who had me and my fellow attorneys shook when it came to the risk of losing at trial. In their courtrooms, if a jury came back with a guilty verdict, those two particular judges would always sentence the defendant to the maximum sentence. So, even if the defendant did not have any priors, despite having discretion to sentence to anything from time-served, through probation, and up to the max, these judges would just always sentence the max. For example, supposed you are borrowing your homeboy's car and you get pulled over for speeding. The officer intimidates you to allow him to search it, and he finds some baggies of crack cocaine under the seat. You are alone in the car, so not only are you arrested for it, but there are no viable motions to suppress the evidence. You have no priors, so the state is offering two years of probation, with the opportunity to early terminate your probation and have it taken off your record after completing a drug treatment program and doing 50 hours of community service. But, to hell with that. It is not your drugs. Surely, you have a good shot at raising a reasonable doubt with the jury at trial. However, if for some reason the jury decides to convict, some judges would sentence you to five years in prison, which is the maximum sentence for a third-degree felony in Florida. You are going to prison and all the horrors that go with that, you are tagged with a felony record, and the judge sleeps like a baby that night.

As a public defender, the lack of empathy and disregard for humanity was infuriating. By having a public defender, such folks were already marked with misfortune by way of their indigent status. There is often a continuance granted between convictions and sentencing, during which time the lawyer puts together mitigation relating to why a lenient sentence is warranted. Experts are retained and family and friends take time off work for sentencing day, where there is much pleading and tears shed. Still, the callous judge does not care. In the legal profession, it is referred to as a "trial tax." It is not an official thing, but it is a real thing in many courthouses. A judge will punish a defendant for having the sheer audacity to exercise his Sixth Amendment right to a jury trial. For the judge, their salary is the same whether they are sitting over a complex multi-week trial or heading home in the early afternoons, while their legal assistant drafts responses to motions. Though there are some good honorable and fair judges in the American criminal justice system, there are not enough. My point here is not to tell you to never take a chance at trial. You have that right. But you must know your judge. Trust your lawyer and do your own research about the judge who will be trying your case.

Another thing to consider when going to sentencing before a judge with so much power is to take the situation gravely serious. Be humble and bring good people to court to speak on your behalf. Speak respectfully and with sincerity. I have seen judges who are generally fair, light up a defendant for being cute or flippant in court during sentencing. Needless to say, but I have seen it, so, do not wear something stupid or disrespectful before the judge such as foul language or disrespectful imagery. Wear your nicest suit. Swallow your pride and respect the power of the court, for your own sake and for your family.

Sentencing is also a time to show your humility and this is on behalf of yourself and others. I have discussed your need to forgive yourself. I sat second-chair for a trial with my girlfriend during my time in the public defender's office. It was a losing case based on aggravated assault against the defendant's girlfriend. I had to handle sentencing, as my girlfriend had to rush home for her grandfather's funeral. The client was looking at about five years in prison, but I was hoping for less and maybe some probation with anger management counseling. The client was angry and difficult, but I learned from his mother that she had abused him severely when he was a small child, before she, herself, got "saved" and sober. The client was too proud to discuss this information, and the mother did not want to talk about it because she did not want to be made to "look bad." He was prideful and stubborn, while the mom was emotionally selfish. Great, based on that combination and with no other witnesses willing and able to offer much mitigation aside from pleading and talking about what a "great guy" the client could become, he wound up being sentenced to what the prosecution requested. Sentencing time is when you must be humble and honest. Some judges are empathetic and willing to show compassion. You must have the courage to give of yourself and expose the reasons behind your scars.

Another point on mental preparation for court reminds me of a Mexican client I had one time. It was an arraignment court day, which means I was meeting him for the first time. As a defense attorney, the point of an arraignment date in the felony division is to meet your client officially for the first time, plead not guilty and determine if the services of the public defender's office are required. Usually the day means that a new court date should be scheduled, or in some rare cases, a trial day is set out far in advance to learn about the case and determine a strategy.

So, when I met this middle-aged gentleman in the jailed bird section otherwise reserved for jurors, I was perplexed when he rejected my introduction and request for another court date with a promise to meet. He only spoke Spanish, so our conversation took place through an interpreter. This man wanted his case resolved that day. He was in felony court for a charge of Driving Under the Influence (DUI) for which he already had three prior convictions. I did my due diligence by asking the prosecutor what they were offering. They wanted him to do four years in prison. My client scoffed at that and said he would take ninety days. What? He insisted on resolving the case that day and said he wanted to plea open to the judge for a better offer.

I spent nearly the entire arraignment proceeding trying to talk him into a continuance. I explained that I knew nothing about his case, and he could maybe have a viable motion to suppress the stop, which could get the whole damn case dismissed. I had two other lawyers attempt to talk some sense into him. None of it worked. He was stubborn, and frankly, foolish.

My client obviously had experience being sentenced for DUI. He was used to getting a small amount of jail time, maybe with some probation and treatment. He was not willing to do more than ninety days in jail and did not want to mess with probation. In sum, he did not want the prosecutor's prison offer, which is understandable, but he also wanted everything resolved in a way that was very irrational. I could not believe that I was about to enter an open plea for a client I did not know, and for a case I knew nothing about. By the time his case was finally called, all I could do was tell the court our predicament and hope the judge could talk the defendant into continuing the case.

For Black Men/Ali Shakoor

The man proved unconvinced of the notion to accept any decision other than throwing himself on the "mercy of the court." I protected myself by annotating the file, and stating on the record, as vigorously as possible while keeping my composure, that his plea was _against the advice of counsel_! All I could do up to that point was gather as much information as I could for mitigation. I told the judge about his background, family obligations, and commitment to change his ways. The prosecution reminded the court that he was a multi-time DUI offender. He therefore had not learned his lesson about the dangers of driving while intoxicated and needed to spend four years in prison; one short of the maximum of five for the third-degree felony. The court gave me the last word, which essentially amounted to begging for leniency and probation with treatment for alcoholism.

The judge took a few moments to go over the minimal documents he had in his possession for the case, and announced his sentence of two years in prison, followed by two years of probation. He "split the baby," as one of the more morbid metaphors in the criminal justice field allows as a description for not giving either side exactly what they want. It could have been worse, but the client stood in a state of shock before being escorted out. Members of his family sobbed in the audience.

Several months later, I received a call from a prospective private attorney who had been contacted by my client's family. Long story short, he wanted to be brought back before the court for a Motion to Withdraw Plea. We never filed an appeal, because his sentence was legal. This is something that I cannot stress enough. Appeals are rarely effective. There must be some indication of clear error by the judge at some point of the legal proceedings and often the error needs to be objected to on the record, in order to preserve the issue. This defendant's sentence was legal and there was no error in the all the mere twenty to thirty minutes we spent on the record for the case. I brought him back to court some time later and spoke with him through an interpreter, to clarify that he was claiming that the initial interpreter "lied" to the judge about his true wishes for a continuance. Also, he was allegedly feeling very ill on the day of the initial sentence and did not believe he was in his right mind to make a decision. Now obviously, the actual trial record and the judge's thorough colloquy asking about his fitness, health, and true desire to plead guilty for a same day sentence, belies what the defendant was saying months after the fact. But the dude had buyer's remorse. He wanted a do over. It did not work that way. It does not work that way. The judge was not buying it, and the private attorney was only willing to jump in if the court reversed itself and withdrew the plea. The defendant was sent back to prison for the remainder of his sentence, followed by a term of probation. Moral of the story, be patient and take the legal process seriously. Respect the power of the court. Allow your defense attorney to fight your case.

Also keep in mind that vile racism in this country infects the bench. There are judges at the county, state, and federal level, who would sentence black people more severely than their fellow whites; everything else related to the crimes being equal other than the race of the defendants. Some of these white judges are just evil racists. Others suffer from bias they may not even recognize, as they see white defendants—fellow members of their tribe—as being more redeemable. Federally, studies have shown black men being sentenced to prison longer than whites, for the exact same crimes. https://www.washingtonpost.com/news/wonk/wp/2017/11/16/black-men-sentenced-to-more-time-for-committing-the-exact-same-crime-as-a-white-person-study-finds/?utm_term=.9fe17cd56ea8

In the courthouse where I once worked as public defender in Hillsborough County, Florida, I've learned of a judge who would allegedly always sentence a black male to longer prison sentences for crimes involving a handgun, while bending over backwards to give white males more lenient sentences. It's been an open secret in the courthouse. It's infuriating and patently unacceptable. Florida has a very serious problem when it comes to disparate treatment in sentencing along racial lines. http://projects.heraldtribune.com/bias/sentencing/ Some white judges will think nothing of throwing a black person away into the state prison industrial complex. Expose racist judges and vote them out of office.

Speaking of exposure to state prison, it is important to understand yourself and your environment prior to accepting a probation deal, as opposed to finishing a sentence in the local county jail and moving on with your freedom. Not everyone is a good candidate for probation, or "paper" as it is often called in our culture. Probation requires being available for and passing random drug/alcohol screening. You must be gainfully employed or actively seeking a job. You cannot be around criminal activity or associate with those who are involved. Sometimes you may have a monitoring device as a requirement that may malfunction, or you may misunderstand how to use it. If you get a "demon" probation officer on a power trip, you may be doomed to fail because the probation officer just wants to get you in violation. Sure, some people can take to probation as a chance to turn their life around and get lucky with a supportive probation officer, while taking advantage of effective counseling and treatment. The worry about violating probation is that it often means a trip to state prison.

I still get frustrated thinking about an older black woman I met sitting in the jail box during a felony court date for violation of probation. She had been locked up for over thirty days for a dirty urine and the prosecutor was offering ninety days to resolve the initial drug possession charge, thereby ending the case. In the alternative, they were willing to continue probation, but with a two-year suspended prison sentence for another violation. Considering the likelihood of gain-time, she could have been released from county jail and free to live her life in another thirty to forty days, maybe less. This defendant was a drug addict who had been in and out of jail in the recent years of her life. She could do the rest of this county time "standing on her head." Nope, she wanted the probation. I tried to plead with her to reconsider. Probation is a trap for a drug addict living in poverty. If she wanted to get clean, finally, why not just finish the county time and take advantage of community resources without prison time hanging over her head? My office could even help her upon release. Nope, she wanted the paper. You know how this case ended. Less than a month later she was back in court for another dirty urine test, which violated her probation. She was basically too embarrassed to make eye contact with me. I was sad to see a woman going to prison and removed from her children and grandbabies, due to a short-sighted decision. Look, you have a right to accept or decline any plea offer that you want. Just understand your predicament. Try to avoid being in the criminal justice system at all costs and limit your exposure to time in the state penitentiary.

Do not talk to the goddamn police in hopes of them looking the other way or protecting you. Assert your Fifth Amendment right to not incriminate yourself. I cannot stress this enough. Once you are arrested, no good ever comes from talking to the men and women in law enforcement. I will never for the life of me understand how or why seasoned career criminals think they can talk their way out of a charge or for a bit of leniency. Often, defendants are talking while drunk or high, and other times these folks are just soberly foolish. This shit is recorded, man. And the officers will be writing copious notes. *"Anything you say, can and will be used against you."* This is legit! Let us say you innocently missed a detail about the time of day or misremember who was present. Law enforcement and the prosecutors will use a seemingly innocent mistake and make you look like a pathological liar. You must not trust them. Officers are trained in techniques of mental manipulation. I have had clearly guilty capital defendants talk in ways that just helped the State prove their case, and men I believe to be factually innocent, get tricked into implicating themselves on felony charges they could not have committed. Do not ever talk to the cops. No good can come of it. Just say one word, *"Lawyer!"*

I also must remind you about the obvious factor that all jail calls are recorded. Do not talk about your case on the phone. You are just providing evidence for the government to use against you. You are not going to be cute and trick anyone into believing any of your perceived exculpatory theories. If you threaten or intimidate any witnesses on the phone, you are only talking yourself into additional charges. The jail staff, an arm of the State, is also usually reading all your personal, non-legal, mail. Do not believe any special code words or innuendo will trick the looming eyes of the government that wants to nail you.

Speaking of communication, if you are getting pulled over for a DUI, and you know you are piss drunk, take the "L" and deal with the arrest. Everything you do or say is simply providing evidence to be used against you. If you talk, the officer can smell the odor of alcohol and detect slurred words. If you try to do the field sobriety exercises, a stumble or unsteady gait will belie your confidence in your perceived steady natural athleticism. The less effective evidence against you for a possible DUI conviction, the more likely you are to get away with a "careless" or "reckless" driving charge. It is expensive for prosecutors to take a case to trial, and they need to secure a conviction beyond and to the exclusion of every reasonable doubt. They are more likely to resolve a case to your satisfaction, if they have less favorable facts for their prosecution. Favorable facts for them are obviously unfavorable and negative facts for defendants. Limit the amount of facts that can be used against you when it comes to DUI investigations. This could mean less criminal liability, less jail exposure, and less of a burden on your insurance rates and finances. Obviously, you should never drive while intoxicated. It is incredibly stupid and dangerous. My point is that understanding the law, and the use of provable facts, is essential to be a free and productive citizen. This book is about keeping you out of jail. The best way to stay out of jail is to abide by the law.

It is crucial to understand your Fourth Amendment right against unreasonable search and seizure. Most police officers do not want to lie and cheat. They rarely even need to because so many citizens do not understand that they have the right to say "no." If an officer is asking your permission to search, that means you have the right to say "no." You may not know if someone borrowed your clothes or left something illegal in your vehicle. Nor do you want to give access to a potential demon cop who may want to plant evidence. Often, I have asked clients why they gave permission to search their body, vehicle, or home, and they usually respond that they think officers will override them and search anyway. Do not be too intimidated to understand and assert your rights. If an officer thinks they have a legal excuse to go into your car or home, they will have a warrant or simply force their way in. Always assert your Fourth Amendment rights.

Do not drive around while smoking a blunt. I have friends that do it. I did it when I was young. It is reckless and stupid. You are putting other people at risk while driving impaired, and also providing police officers with a justifiably legal stop and search of your vehicle. Obviously, we know weed has a distinct smell and that odor gives officers probable cause to search. Some problems are completely avoidable.

Also, regarding drug possession, it is important to understand sentencing enhancements and prison exposure when it comes to possessing certain quantities. Whether we are talking weed, cocaine/crack, heroin, LSD or pills, you need to understand that you should not possess or sell drugs, and large amounts can particularly ruin your life. Do not take the chance.

We as black people must be conscientious to overcome the high hurdles and moving goalposts put down in front of us by oppressive white supremacy. You can and must be readily capable for the fight, but I know it is not an easy task. I want you to master the laws pertaining to street crime, just as certain demographics use savvy intellect in navigating the laws of securities fraud, tax evasion, money laundering and other white-collar crimes. Everyone should understand our constitutional rights. The U.S. Constitution, this great and powerful American document, applies to every damn one of us. Learn the law and always assert your constitutional rights. Take pride in your knowledge and freedom. Lastly, do not break the law.

For Black Men/Ali Shakoor

Chapter Ten

Walking and Thinking

Now that you have, thus far, endured everything that life has thrown at you, take a minute to give proper respect to the fact that you are still alive. If you are free in this world, and you are not going into prison, because you have made sound judgment or by good fortune, then this is splendid. If you have been there before, or are in prison right at this moment, understand, you know you are not going back. You do not have to accept defeat to understand the reality that our people cannot defeat the power of white supremacy in our lifespan. Racism is ingrained in America; from the moment we were brought here as property. Jim Crow was not very long ago at all, as black folks who survived it and whites that directly profited from it are alive today. Some white folks resent the gains we've made. And every white person has had a dearly beloved relative or close family friend who is an abhorrent racist in their lifetime. So many white folks compartmentalize and rationalize bigotry, while benefitting from the evils of institutional racism. Also consider the white people who simply don't see or understand what happen to black Americans, as they fight through their own personal struggles. It is up to us to maintain our sanity, vote and fight for justice with like-minded people. Oppressive white supremacy will forever be a part of America, because despite the progress made over the years, it's just too deeply rooted in America's fabric to be eradicated. But you can control how you react to it. You can survive and thrive in this country. Do not feel defeated. Control what you can, which starts with dictating your own actions and leading a productive life.

Join the varied cultures within America who really want nothing more than freedom and justice. Do not allow oppressors and oppression to destroy you. Take control of yourself and of how you react to struggles in life. Do so with the knowledge that you can navigate and fight through everything they try to do to us. You are not going to be a distraction or cautionary tale for them to deflect to. Our people are strong, and we exude greatness, so become a great man with the highest standards.

I have given you nine chapters of reflection and advice in this book. This is all based on my personal and professional experiences. I am writing with deep love for our people. Here in this final chapter, we have come full circle to the first chapter's lesson of self-love. It is important to love yourself and your place in this world. Take a walk.

Take a walk in your town during the daytime. Feel the energy of the sun. Understand why our Richard Pryor's *"Mudbone"* talked about getting some sunshine on your face. Get out and feel the energy of the sun and breathe in the air. Life is a blessing. Freedom cannot be taken for granted. Walk the streets and look at the people. Gather in the images of the communities; the ones you escaped from, the ones you want to see improved, and the areas you plan to eventually settle into for the next stage of your life as a free man. Let the sun charge you up like a battery. Burn away your tendencies toward poor choices and let the best version of yourself shine bright. You should take advantage of everything the sun gives us. Accept what you deserve from the blessings of the sun. Breathe in the air and feel inspired by the fact that you are free and alive.

Sometime during the early night, take a walk. Do it after the sun goes down, so you can see the stars decorating the sky. Find a safe area to stroll under the moonlight. Think of everything in your life that you have overcome and appreciate how damn strong you are. Forgive yourself for all of your past poor choices. Suppress any tendencies toward sabotage. You are a new man. Just take a moment to feel yourself. Life is a miracle, a blessing. You're a good man. Value and love yourself. Walk along a safe pathway toward your destination. Make sure you can see clearly. Do not get lost in the darkness. Stay in the light.

For Black Men Trying to Survive and Thrive in America

A Defense Attorney's Advice and Life Experiences

<u>About the Author</u>

Ali Andrew Shakoor is a post-conviction attorney with over 15 years of experience in the criminal law field. He has argued cases before the Florida Supreme Court and the United States Court of Appeals for the Eleventh Circuit. He received his Juris Doctor degree, *cum laude*, from Capital University Law School in Columbus, Ohio. Ali is a proud 'Buckeye.' He earned his B.A. at The Ohio State University with a major in Political Science and minors in Women's Studies and Black Studies. Ali served as a volunteer for Big Brothers Big Sisters of America. He is politically active and has volunteered on many national and local political campaigns. Ali is passionate about social justice. He loves sports-particularly boxing and the NBA. He lives in Tampa, Florida.

This is Ali Shakoor's first book.